THE

MYTHS *of*

MARRIAGING

FAMILIUS

All author proceeds and royalties from this book go Eyrealm, a Public Charity, which helps third-world families and offers free parenting and family strengthening ideas to all. You are invited to Eyrealm's website at Family.Is and its social media pages: "Family Is" on Instagram and Twitter, and "My Family" on Facebook.

Published by Familius LLC, www.familius.com

Familius books are available at special discounts for bulk purchases, whether for sales promotions or for family or corporate use. For more information, contact Familius Sales at 559-876-2170 or email orders@familius.com.

Library of Congress Cataloging-in-Publication Data
2019935082

Print ISBN 9781641701396
Ebook ISBN 9781641702041

Printed in the United States of America

Edited by Kaylee Mason, Michele Robbins, and Alison Strobel
Cover design by Derek George
Book design by Brooke Jorden

10 9 8 7 6 5 4 3 2 1

First Edition

THE

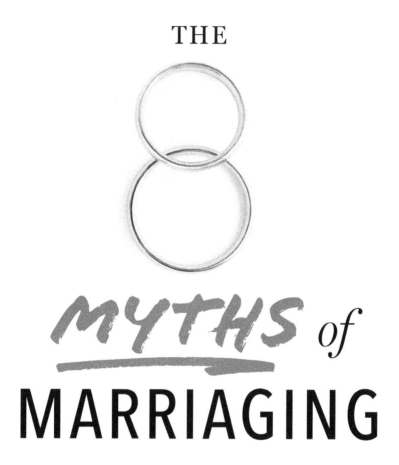

MYTHS *of*

MARRIAGING

MAKING MARRIAGE A VERB
AND REPLACING MYTH WITH
TRUTH

NEW YORK TIMES #1 BESTSELLING AUTHORS

RICHARD & LINDA EYRE

To our four daughters-in-law—Aja, Anita, Kristi, and Julie—
and our four sons-in-law—Jared, David, Jeff, and Ian—
who have introduced us to a whole new world
of varied possibilities for marriage and have brightened and
broadened our children in the process.

Released on the day of their 50th wedding anniversary, this is the first and only book on marriage that prolific, bestselling family and parenting authors Richard and Linda Eyre have ever written.

"We didn't want to tackle this subject," says Linda, "until we had five decades of it under our belts."

ACKNOWLEDGMENTS

With gratitude for our favorite publishing company Familius, a company led by Christopher Robbins a unique and gifted publisher and friend who shares our passion for making families better—and happier. We are also grateful to Brooke Jorden for her design, management, and editing, and also to Kaylee Mason and Michelle Robbins whose edits and suggestions have made this a better book!

Marriaging is a never-ending process! How we appreciate our children who have shown us new ideas and paths through their own marriage processes and our friends from Inklngs, our forty-year-old literary group whose stellar and vastly different but inspirational marriages have helped us in our thinking and writing. They have worked with us to discover the myths and refine the truths of marriage!

CONTENTS

(AKA: A PREVIEW OR EXECUTIVE SUMMARY)

We want you to see where this book is going before it takes you there, so this is not a spoiler but an appetizer. The eight myths, each with a hint of the opposite and corresponding truth, are listed as a general table of contents and as teasers. (When you get to each section, you will find that there are sub-myths and sub-truths as well.)

PREFACE xi

INTRODUCTION: THE DANGER OF MYTHS 1

1. THE CLONE MYTH 5

MYTH: A good measure of the quality of your relationship or marriage is how alike you are and how infrequently you disagree or argue.

TRUTH: Some of the best and most exciting marriages are between two strong individuals who relish rather than resent their differences; who each have their own unique opinions and can disagree and debate and learn from each other. "How you resolve" is a better measure than "how often you need to."

(And other myths and truths about alikeness and agreement.)

2. THE ACHIEVEMENT MYTH 25

MYTH: Achievements are harder and take more work than relationships do.

TRUTH: Relationships are, both in the short term and the long term, always more important than achievements—and usually harder.

(And other myths and truths about priorities.)

3. THE INDEPENDENCE MYTH 55

MYTH: It is best for each spouse to maintain his or her own independence and to form a self-reliant two-way partnership.
TRUTH: Independence is overrated and lonely; and it gets more so the longer we live. Interdependence is the acknowledgment of this simple, vulnerable truth, and it is a joy to willingly, enthusiastically trade your independence for interdependence. Ultimately, a three-way partnership that recognizes dependence on God is the strongest of all.

(And other myths and truths about freedom.)

4. THE PERFECTION MYTH 75

MYTH: I can find (or create) a perfect match for myself and then I will be happy.
TRUTH: Some married couples are better matched than others; there are even those who believe they have found their soul mate. But most marriages are about accommodation and adjustment—and more about changing our own minds than about fixing our spouse's.

(And other myths and truths about happiness and expectations.)

5. THE NO-WAVES MYTH 95

MYTH: In marriage, some things are better left unsaid; and it's safest to float along and not make waves.
TRUTH: Unexpressed feelings never die; they are just buried and come forth later in uglier forms. Timing is important, but the best marriages communicate everything—even when it creates some turbulence.

(And other myths and truths about marital communication.)

6. THE TEST-DRIVE MYTH 121

MYTH: You wouldn't buy a car until you had taken a test drive, and it is unwise to make a marriage commitment before you have lived together long enough to know if it will work.
TRUTH: It is the commitment that will make a marriage work. Real security comes from promising and implementing complete allegiance, not from conditional, tentative try-it-and-see.

(And other myths and truths about commitment.)

7. THE EQUALITY MYTH 151

MYTH: Equality should be the prime goal of your relationship or your marriage.

TRUTH: Striving for equality breeds comparing and criticism, and it may produce more competition than compatibility. It is better to work for a marriage of synergistic "oneness" that breeds cooperation and compensates for one another's weaknesses.

(And other myths and truths about sameness.)

8. THE MYTH OF MARRIAGE'S DEMISE 171

MYTH: Marriage is on the decline and is weakening and disappearing as an institution.

TRUTH: The strongest, most fulfilling marriages in the history of the world exist today.

(And other myths and truths about the macro of marriage in society.)

AFTERWORD:
A PERSONAL AFFIRMATION FROM THE EYRES 197

The View from Here
(Looking forward and back after fifty years.)

APPENDIX A:
A SHORT Q&A INTERVIEW WITH *SUCCESS MAGAZINE* 211

APPENDIX B: BOOK GROUP QUESTIONS 217

NOTES 219

ABOUT THE AUTHORS 223

OTHER FAMIILIUS BOOKS BY THE EYRES 224

ABOUT FAMILIUS 228

MARRIAGING IS ALWAYS WORTH THE EFFORT

We call it "marriaging" because it is a dynamic, happening word; while "marriage" is a static, happened word. Marriaging, like parenting, is a skill—or an art or a science—that can be continually and actively worked on, developed, and improved.

We will use this new word "marriaging" throughout the book and you will know its proactive, working-to-get-better meaning. *Marriage* is the noun, but *marriaging* is the verb. As we strive to get better at it, we want the ability to say "I'm marriaging" just like we say "I'm parenting."

As we strive to build and grow our marriaging ability, there are some misconceptions that can get in our way—some misplaced beliefs or false paradigms that point us in the wrong directions and suck the joy out of our relationships. They do this through unrealistic expectations and false goals that cause dissatisfaction, discouragement, and frustration.

We call these misconceptions the Myths of

> **Marriaging, like parenting, is a skill that can be continually and actively worked on, developed, and improved.**

Marriaging. They all sound good—many of them are even disguised as wise advice or packaged as sage insights. Indeed we may have heard some of them so many times that we assume they must be true.

But they are not.

Some of these myths raise our hopes and expectations unreasonably; others oversimplify; and still others exaggerate a good direction so much that it turns back and harms our relationship instead.

The good news is that wherever there is a myth there is a countering truth. There is another side of the coin—the true side.

Sometimes knowing both sides, and considering them together, can clarify and illuminate. Sometimes we need first to know what *not* to do or think or believe in order to avoid the common pitfalls that often overtake a marriage.

Then, by contrast, we need to know what *to* do or think or believe in order to maximize our marriages.

So we will first try to dispel the myths, then to capture the truths.

A myth is a mist;

A truth is a trumpet.

The mist is deceptive, disingenuous, and dangerous;

The truth is clear, loud, and unmistakable.

And beyond the sorting out of myths and truths,

We need practical ideas to emerge from one and implement the other.

What we all need is clear directions and goals because:

Marriage is not a stationary thing.

It is always moving and changing,

And to keep moving in the right direction,

It needs a lot of refreshing,

A lot of fresh approaches,

A lot of new oxygen!

This takes effort, but it is effort well-expended because good marriaging is the best path to a healthy family and a happy life.

When we speak or lead discussions, we often begin by asking our audiences what really matters in life. We get some interesting answers that range from the practical to the ethereal, from the conceptual to the crass. Some of the most common answers are:

- Peace
- Satisfaction
- Investments
- Achievements
- Reputation
- Comfort

But the number one answer—every time—is:

- Relationships.

After we get these responses, we love expressing our belief that marriage is not only the prime relationship but the epitome and the source of all the other hopes and desires they have just listed.

A strong stable marriage is the most lasting source of peace.

The satisfaction of a lifetime love surpasses all others.

What we invest in the institution of marriage

pays the highest dividends and the best overall return of all.

Compared to the achievement of a lasting marriage,

all other accomplishments pale,

because it is not just an achievement or an accomplishment,

it is a relationship.

And there is no better relationship

And no stronger reputation

than that of a genuine, lasting marriage.

And as years pass,

the only reliable comfort is in this union.

Richard and Linda Eyre,
Park City, Utah, on July 30, 2019 (Our fiftieth anniversary)

PS—Immanuel Kant waited until his old age to publish his key works of philosophy because he didn't feel like he knew enough before that.

We waited until our fiftieth anniversary to write our first book on marriage for the same reason.

And even now we feel like we may know more about what not to do in marriaging than what to do. We suppose that is why we call this book *The Eight Myths of Marriaging.*

And keep in mind that even after fifty years, nothing is completely safe or guaranteed.

We heard a story of a Canadian couple being interviewed on the occasion of their eightieth anniversary. She was 98 and he was 101, and before the interviewer could ask his first question the husband said, "There is something you should know, we are getting a divorce."

The interviewer couldn't believe his ears. "You're getting a divorce?" he exclaimed. "After eighty years?"

"Yes," said the old fellow. "We wanted to wait until all the kids were dead."

So whatever your age and however long you have been married (or if you are just contemplating the possibility) let's remember that marriage is never simple and never easy. However, it is always worth the thought and effort we put into it.

> Immanuel Kant waited until his old age to publish his key works of philosophy because he didn't feel like he knew enough before that.
>
> We waited until our fiftieth anniversary to write our first book on marriage for the same reason.

PPS—A quick comment on the word *myth*, which has two meanings. The older is "an unprovable story that emphasizes the deepest questions and best answers that illustrate the foundational values of a particular cultural or tradition." The newer meaning is "a phony story often unquestioningly believed."

Obviously, it is the second kind of myth that we are trying to expose here—*false* myths about marriaging. These unquestioned beliefs influence our general culture in a harmful way.

But it is good to remember that there are *true* marriage myths too. Beliefs—historical or not—that emphasize the powerful reality of committed long-term, hardworking, difficult-but-joyful marriage provide our culture with alternative true myths to the false myths that we challenge in this book.

PPPS—Just a suggestion, but, if you can, read this book with your spouse—out loud. We promise it will prompt discussion and, at times, a new level of communication.

If you can't do that with the whole book, then as you read separately, mark the parts that you want to re-read later together.

INTRODUCTION

THE DANGER OF MYTHS

Here is the problem with myths: They cause us to see ourselves and our world unrealistically and to want things that will never happen—or that might be bad for us if they did.

Unrealistic wants lead to dissatisfaction, discouragement, and frustration when we can't get what we think we should have. Or the reverse may occur—when a myth tells us that things are not possible when they really are, causing us to accept mediocrity and to disengage from our dreams.

Myths of false ideals set us off in the pursuit of the wrong things or deter us from the pursuit of the right things.

Myths can blind us to the good and the possible and cause us to miss the best moments and the best opportunities.

However, if we can shove the myths aside, we will blast through the misconceptions that are making us unhappy in our marriages and then reveal hidden joys.

So here is a rundown of the eight marriage myths and what they do to us:

1. *The Clone Myth* makes us wish for constant agreement and alikeness—which would actually narrow and dull our marriages; and it causes us to resent and be discouraged with the very differences that can bring growth and excitement.

2. *The Achievement Myth* channels our energy toward things and away from people, causing us to seek the accolades and acknowledgment of achievement more than the love and sacrifice of relationships; and perhaps to work harder at parenting than at marriaging.

3. *The Independence Myth* blocks unity and hides our vulnerability under a blanket of pride. This causes us to refuse to admit our need for each other and to fail to accept the beauty of interdependence with each other and dependence on God.

4. *The Perfection Myth* makes us more aware of and more irritated by our spouse's faults and too aware of our own needs and unaware of our partner's happiness.

5. *The No-Waves Myth* deceives us into hiding things from our spouse and smoothing over the rough edges that could give our marriage texture and grit; and it bottles up feelings that irritate, fester, and breed dissatisfaction.

6. *The Test-Drive Myth* breeds criticism and judgment and encourages us to try to preserve all our options rather than make the very commitment that could make us more resilient and forgiving.

7. *The Equality Myth* pushes us to compare and compete, to resent our spouse's roles and opportunities, and to feel frustrated with our own lack of success. It also makes us more aware of our partner's weaknesses and undermines the possibilities for synergy and for complementing one another's strengths and compensating for each other's weaknesses.

8. *The Myth of Marriage's Demise* discourages us and drains away our hope for society, making us feel like misfits or dinosaurs in our own pursuit of a committed, lasting marriage.

This book will take you through the eight myths one at a time—like stepping from one rock to the next in crossing a stream—and then it will expose, expel, and excise them, because . . .

One of the best ways to grasp and understand a truth is to explode the myth that opposes or blocks it. Only when the mists of a myth clear away can we see and hear the trumpet of the truth that it was hiding.

One reason marriage is discredited, discarded, and declining across society today is that too many believe these eight myths and are distracted, discouraged, and deterred by them.

These myths are all somewhat subtle and nuanced—often containing a half-truth—and each casts a spell that is easy to fall under. Dispelling (or dis-spell-ing) them is the best way we know to move past them and find better, truer paradigms.

We will couple each myth with its corresponding truth, and each of the eight sections will have separately numbered chapters, so the first chapter relating to the first myth will be 1-1 and the first chapter of the second myth will be 2-1.

We hope you enjoy (and are somewhat relieved by) the discrediting of the eight myths; we hope you are refreshed by the exploration of their replacement truths.

One reason marriage is discredited, discarded, and declining across society today is that too many believe these eight myths and are distracted, discouraged, and deterred by them.

1. The Clone Myth

(AND OTHER MYTHS AND TRUTHS ABOUT ALIKENESS AND AGREEMENT.)

MYTH: A good measure of the quality of your relationship or marriage is how alike you are and how infrequently you disagree or argue.

TRUTH: The best and most exciting marriages are between strong individuals who relish rather than resent their differences; who each have their own unique opinions and can disagree, debate, and learn from each other. "How you resolve" is a better measure than "how often you need to."

1. **SUB-MYTH: It is important to "never let the sun set on a disagreement"; every conflict must be resolved.**

   TRUTH: If a disagreement is spiraling out of control, it's better to put it on hold and revise your motto to: "Never let the week end without talking through and understanding any lingering concerns." And loving, committed relationships can be maintained despite unresolved differences.

2. **SUB-MYTH: Wanting my spouse to "complete me" is a realistic hope for marriage.**

   TRUTH: You should work to complete yourself and should support your spouse in that same personal quest.

3. **SUB-MYTH: The more you disagree, the worse your marriage gets and the less likely you are to ever get in sync.**

   TRUTH: Marital conflict resolution or mutual understanding is a growing process and a learned skill, and there are three basic methods that are almost always helpful.

4. **SUB-MYTH: Children should never see their parents disagree.**

   TRUTH: Children need to know that their parents are two separate individuals who sometimes have different opinions. It's okay if they see you disagree, but they also need to see you resolve and make up.

1-1: GOOD A'S AND BAD D'S?

We got married in the summer of 1969, exactly one week after Neil Armstrong took one small step on the moon. It was a turbulent time with a war in Vietnam and all kinds of protests and upheavals at home. But we viewed our marriage as the calm center of the hurricane, sure that our love would produce ever greater peace and harmony in our personal lives.

It didn't take us long to wake up. We married in Utah and our honeymoon was our drive to graduate school in Boston. We rode along in Linda's massive Ford Galaxie, pulling Richard's bathtub Porsche disguised as a trailer and crammed full of all our earthly belongings. During those five days on the road, we discovered countless ways we were different from each other and countless subjects on which we disagreed. The smooth lovely bubble of our courtship burst, and we entered the rough and real world of merging two very different lives. There were times on that drive when we thought we should turn around and other times when we thought we had better unhook the Porsche and set off in the opposite direction.

Most of us assume, at least early in our relationship, that the D's are bad and the A's are good. That is, *agreement* and being *alike* are good; *disagreement* and *differences* are bad. But the whole concept is a myth.

Compatibility is a learned skill and—particularly for two strong-willed, opinionated people—it never comes easily. And when we think the route to it is to become clones of each other and to view the whole world in exactly the same way, we are not only kidding ourselves, but we are shortchanging ourselves and underestimating the power, purpose, and pleasure of being different. Often, being different leads to finding a third way that is better than either of the original ones.

We run across so many couples who think that the goal is to be alike and in agreement all the time. But this is a myth that brings discouragement and guilt and that undermines happiness.

In fact, those two A's may be the worst measurements of marriage that we know.

These are some far better yardsticks of progress:

- Is your spouse happy?
- Are you both growing?
- Do you feel always loved?
- Do you feel accepted for who you are?
- Who do you turn to for emotional needs? Who is your best friend?
- Can you be completely honest and completely yourself with your spouse?
- How deep is your commitment?
- Can you disagree without being threatened and build those disagreements into harmony?
- Can you differ from your spouse without feeling worry or failure and build those differences into synergy?

So, let's begin by changing our measurements and appreciating our diversity and differences.

The best marriaging occurs when partners continue to progress as who they are; in fact some differences may actually get larger, expanding the possibilities for synergy. Differences that combine and complement each other add up to a lot more than two people trying to clone each other.

If you and your spouse were perfectly alike, there would be no dynamic tension, no need to debate or resolve or come together, and very little excitement.

If you and your spouse were perfectly alike, there would be no dynamic tension, no need to debate or resolve or come together, and very little excitement.

> *My barber, who I go to as much for the conversation as for the haircut, says it this way: "If my husband had married someone just like himself it would have been the most boring marriage ever, and if I had married someone just like me it would have been constant pandemonium. He keeps my feet on the ground and I keep his head in the clouds."*

The Gottman Institute's research on successful couples shows that happy, long-term marriages never actually achieve full agreement on the majority of their conflicts. Therefore, in this book whenever we use the term "conflict resolution," we are referring either to agreement, compromise, or an amical ability to understand and respect each other's viewpoint. Successful couples learn to sustain and even improve their marriage relationship by re-engaging their honest disagreements from time to time, while soothing each other with a re-commitment to their loving marriage. This authentic exchange demonstrates the truth that loving trust is more powerful than the need to resolve every disagreement once and for all. The power of trustworthy love is proven and enhanced in the crucible of conflict—if the couple treats each other the right way in the face of disagreements.

1-2: WHY YOU DON'T WANT YOUR MARRIAGE TO BE CONFLICT FREE

Richard: *Many years ago, I was on a plane and happened to be sitting by a distinguished-looking British fellow who told me that he had been a marriage counselor for more than forty years. He mentioned that during all that time he had discovered only three kinds of marriages that were completely conflict free.*

Interested, I grabbed my pencil and notebook and asked him what they were.

"The first kind of conflict-free marriage is one in which one of the two parties is totally dominant and domineering, and the other is such a doormat that there is never any disagreement," I remember him saying. "One just calls all the shots and makes all the decisions, and the other one just goes along."

That discouraged me a little, but I still had hope for the other two.

"The second kind of conflict-free marriage," he said, "is becoming much more common these days. It occurs when two people have basically a marriage of convenience. They live such separate lives and have such separate careers and schedules that they really don't have anything in common to disagree on or have conflict over."

By that point, I couldn't wait to hear what the third type would be.

"The third kind of conflict-free marriage," he said, "is where either the husband or the wife is dead."

He obviously had a droll, English sense of humor, because he said it with a straight face.

I didn't know how to respond, so I just stared at him. He then hammered home his point.

"I mean it," he said. "In all my years of marriage counseling, those are the only three kinds of marriage where there is never a conflict or an argument. So unless you want one of those, you better have some other way of measuring your marriage than an idealistic notion that you must always agree with each other."

We have thought and written a lot about that little conversation over the years and have come to the conclusion that the man was right. In fact, we have concluded that the best way to measure a marriage is not how often there is disagreement, but rather how differences are resolved and how much is learned from them.

As some good friends of ours say, "Communication breakdowns can bring communication breakthroughs." Of course "can" is the operative word. It takes real effort to turn differences into synergy.

But whatever age you are, and whatever age your marriage is, don't be discouraged or dismayed by your occasional disagreements.

We often think of a great and wise mentor of ours who was ninety-five years old when we asked him the secret to his longevity. He thought for a moment and then said, "Well, way back nearly seventy years ago when my wife and I were married, we made a solemn pledge that we would never fight or argue within the walls of our home."

That was interesting, but we thought he had missed our question. But then, with a twinkle in his eye, he continued, "That's how I've lived so long—spent so much time in the out of doors!"

Instead of worrying about disagreeing, worry about resolving differences positively.

So instead of worrying about disagreeing, worry about resolving differences positively. And instead of worrying if your children see you disagreeing (hopefully not violently or angrily), just be sure they also see you resolving things and making up.

It can actually be a problem when children think their parents never argue or differ on anything, because it gives them unrealistic expectations for their own marriages. It's much better for children to know that their parents are each individuals and that they sometimes differ—but that they always work things out and learn together.

All real marriaging has disagreements—the important thing is how we resolve them and grow from them. Unity does not imply a total absence of differences or personal opinions. In fact, it is the differences, dealt with in harmony, that makes marriage both interesting and growth-oriented. A marriage is successful based on how those differences are used, addressed, and resolved.

1-3: THE THREE BEST METHODS OF CONFLICT RESOLUTION

After delivering a speech once, we had a young couple come to us and say, "There must be something really wrong with our marriage because we have only been married a year and we had our first disagreement last week."

We said, "Wow, your first one? After a year? Yes, something must be wrong if you haven't had more arguments than that."

Keep in mind, as we said in Chapter 1-1, that "resolution," can mean agreement, compromise, or an amical ability to understand and respect each other's viewpoint.

There are three methods of conflict resolution that seem to always have a positive effect in marriaging, and they are so simple that they can be stated in three sentences:

1. Rogerian Technique: Have a rule that you must paraphrase back whatever your spouse has just said—to his or her satisfaction—before you can make your own next point. This will force you to really listen to and understand each other.

2. Go to the Balcony: If an argument starts escalating, call a timeout. Each of you can "go to the balcony," meaning take a little walk, change clothes, or do something else for ten to fifteen minutes. During this time you can each reset and

get a bigger perspective, and then reconvene when you are both calmer and more collected.

3. Sunday Session: Have a private meeting or Sunday Session together each week where you review the past week, plan the next week, and "clear the air" of any bad feelings or unresolved differences from the previous week.

Simple but not easy!

The lovely older man who performed our marriage gave us one piece of advice, and it was so beautifully phrased and so idealistic that we embraced it immediately.

"Never let the sun set on a disagreement."

Okay, we thought, we will resolve anything and every-thing—every day. We will never go to bed mad. If we have a conflict, we will solve it and nip it in the bud!

Dream on! In fact, we didn't do much dreaming early in our marriage because we were often arguing into the night. To say the least, the pretty adage about the sun setting was not working. But we finally realized that we didn't have to totally reject the advice—just modify it. We changed it to: "Never let the week end without resolving any arguments from the week passed."

We began the habit of having a private "feelings meeting" each Sunday where we would tell each other about our week and express our feelings for life and for each other. In that mellow and compat-ible atmosphere, with the ground rule of rephrasing each thing the other said before making our next point, we were generally able to bring up and resolve any loose ends that had unraveled a bit during the week.

It wasn't perfect, but it got us back on the same page quickly enough that we were never in different chapters, and it brought into play all three of the best conflict resolution methods we know.

There are two additional methods of conflict resolution to fall back on, particularly when the Rogerian Technique, going to the balcony, and having a Sunday Session don't cut it:

1. PRAYER

Many times, after clashing and disagreeing—each making our own point with conviction, both feeling increasingly sure that we were right—and being just at the point when we felt the least like opening our souls to a higher power, we have been, as Abraham Lincoln wrote, "driven to our knees by the overwhelming conviction that there was nowhere else to go."

Feeling humble and talking to a third party rather than to each other can change the whole chemistry of a disagreement. (And when that third party is divine, your chances of mutual understanding and resolution go way, way up.)

Feeling humble and talking to a third party rather than to each other can change the whole chemistry of a disagreement.

Irrespective of the nature of our faith, those of us who believe in some form of higher power can avail ourselves of higher help by some form of prayer. The atmosphere can change as if there were a warm blanket thrown across the two of you, and you can go from "please help this stubborn person to realize that he is wrong" to "please forgive me for being so strong-willed and not working hard enough to really understand what is in my partner's mind."

2. THERAPY

Working with differences of opinion, wants, and needs, and under-standing each other's viewpoint is sometimes excruciatingly hard work and is often beyond a married couple's ability without outside help. Sometimes that means finding someone who is more knowl-edgeable, who can be more objective, and who can see the problem from an outside vantage point.

Michelle Obama has been eloquent on the subject of knowing when you need help and finding someone who can provide that help. In an interview with ABC news, she said: "I know too many young couples who struggle and think that somehow there's some-thing wrong with them. And I want them to know that Michelle and Barack Obama—who have a phenomenal marriage and who love each other—we work on our marriage. And we get help with our marriage when we need it."[1]

Because of our books and family-centric writing, we are often asked for help on marital issues that we quickly realize are beyond our training and expertise. When this happens, we often suggest marriage counseling from a trained therapist. Getting help when you need it never means you're weak, it shows your strength.

1-4: RELISH RATHER THAN RESENT YOUR DIFFERENCES

Linda: *Richard is the perfect combination of a type A, "go, do, accomplish" personality and a laid-back guru who spends lots of time in the forest, listening for ideas and answers to questions. Nothing in life stresses him out except for issues of safety (an accident over which he has no control), health concerns (something going wrong with a bodily function over which he has no control), and when his favorite basketball team is not doing well (again, something over which he has no control). Exercise is critical to his well-being, and he finds it a delight. Relaxing is also of ultimate importance to him.*

I have a different bunch of things that create stress for me. I stress over pulling off events that loom large—like a big family or friend gathering that I feel needs to be done a certain way, preparing for a big speaking tour, or finishing a book by a deadline. For me, exercise is a chore and not a delight. Additionally, I have a hard time not feeling as though watching sports—unless it's the fourth quarter or last inning and the score is close—is pretty much a waste of time. Dropping my "to do" list and throwing fate to the wind in order to leave it all behind and relax feels more like fingernails on a chalkboard to me.

The rub comes when one or the other of us is stressed about something that seems unimportant or even silly to the other. In the best-case scenario, we calm each other with logic. But when that doesn't work, there is a big bang—or should I say, a colorful clash?

What is a couple to do if they love each other but are very different and frequently find that they are bothered by things the other person does? Maybe one spouse is a detail person and wants everything just right while the other just glosses over things. Or one is neat, fastidious, and orderly while the other is a little sloppy and doesn't mind a certain degree of chaos. Or maybe it's as simple as one thinking the other talks too much, exaggerates, is too shy, or doesn't have strong enough opinions. The list of "things that bother" can be endless!

But let's say that this couple wants unity in their marriaging— they want oneness, they want complete compatibility, and they don't want to bury things and have them fester. So, what do they do?

Do they fight it out every time? Do they just agree to disagree whenever a conflict comes up? Do they each make a list of things that bother them and try to resolve what's on the list once a week? Do they try to understand that doing things differently could be a strength if they can learn to just accept and appreciate each other more? Do they seek a counselor to try to help them be more alike or at least to get on the same page?

Some or all of these may help, but remember this: sameness is not the goal. The strongest unions are not created by two people who are totally alike or who could be clones of each other. As we have discovered, there are productive ways to agree to disagree— not on important values or principles but on certain viewpoints, issues, or ways of doing things. It's diversity, different perspectives, and complementing abilities that create the true synergy of a great marriage.

The challenge is in trying to blend differences, not in trying to make them disappear. Of course, we need to be on the same page as our spouse as much as possible on the big important things—like our goals and our core beliefs. But when it comes to our style, our interests, or our methods and ways of going about things—and to our talents, gifts, and natural abilities—there is a lot of room for difference and uniqueness. Simply put, we need to overcome the natural tendency to want our spouse to "be more like me."

We heard a story about a couple who decided to each make a list of "things I would like to change about you." Predictably, the feelings and outcomes of this were not good.

> *Richard: I came to a realization a few years ago—or maybe I should say I came to a decision—that "I would not change a single thing about Linda." This did not mean I thought Linda was perfect in every way. For example, I do wish she could send shorter texts and that she would answer her phone when I call her. But it meant I had realized that Linda is a complex and internally connected individual and that if one little thing I didn't particularly like was changed, it might create a kind of chain reaction that would also change something I dearly love about her.*
>
> *Linda, to be honest, has not quite come to this same conclusion about me—because I have a lot more rough edges than she does. But we are both getting closer to being able to not only accept our differences but relish them and realize that they constitute much of what we love about each other.*

So here is the challenge: Learn to differentiate between the things that are "just who your spouse is" (things that are "him being him" or "her being her") and the things that really do bother you. Usually, as people think about that differentiation, they are able to move many things from the second category to the first.

1-5: WHAT IS THE GOAL?

Benjamin Franklin put it this way: "After all, wedlock is the natural state of man. A bachelor is not a complete human being. He is like the odd half of a pair of scissors, which has not yet found its fellow, and therefore is not even half so useful as they might be together."

Poll after public opinion poll reveal that married persons are happier than those unmarried. Not only that, but married folks are healthier, more satisfied with life, and live longer. Marriage can create a state of commitment and of contentment that is absent in single life.

Marriaging is never perfect, but married individuals develop more of the characteristics and the character that are associated with personal growth and that point in the direction of personal progression. Marriage partners, even in less-than-ideal unions, compensate for each other's weaknesses. They comfort and support each other, and they create a kind of synergy where the total is more than the sum of its parts.

Marriage is the natural state of affairs.

Of course, there are many who fit in the category of wanting to be married but have yet to find the right person or have the right person find them. We believe their time will come. Our spiritual belief is that everyone will have the opportunity—sometime, either now or in the hereafter—for marriage and family.

It's two other categories that we worry about:

1. Those who are married and wish they were not (though of course not all marriages can or should be saved), and

2. Those who are not married and deliberately plan to keep it that way.

Frankly, these days we meet a lot of people in both of these categories. They say things like:

- "It's just not for me."
- "I'm more of a solitary person."
- "It's just not working."
- "I don't think I could ever find a person who could live with me."
- "I've got a dog, and that is all I need."
- "Honestly, marriage is just too hard; it's more than I can handle."
- "It wouldn't fit with my lifestyle or my life goals."
- "I just don't think I'm ready for the responsibility."
- "I didn't know what I was doing or what I wanted when I married, and it has never worked."

Or perhaps the worst and most depressing sentiment of all:

- "I've seen a lot of marriages and, to be blunt, I wouldn't want any of them. Marriage takes away your individuality."

Wait a minute. What is the message here? Are people saying that happiness is all about ease and lack of responsibility and commitment? Are they saying that loving yourself and being an independent individual is more important than love, commitment, sacrifice, teamwork, or trying to find something bigger and better than self?

Come to think of it, there is a third category we worry about:

3. Those who are married but think of marriage as a loose or convenient relationship that meets a few of each other's needs but doesn't really create a new entity or partnership that is more important than everything else.

We don't think ideal marriaging is when two people have everything in common or where both have the same qualities, temperaments, and perspectives. Again, why would you want to live with a clone of yourself?

Rather, the most exciting and powerful marriaging usually brings together two people with different strengths, gifts, and skills. The two combine to create a new entity that has all of the things that both brought to the table (or to the altar). Then on top of that the two develop even more combined qualities, producing something much more complete than either could have ever become on their own.

Don't long for a frictionless marriage of endless agreement and sameness; seek instead for the ever-interesting and ever-challenging marriage of new combinations and mutual appreciation.

> We decided to think of it as a numbers game. Imagine something that we will call the ACH index—a form of life-measurement standing for Achievement, Contribution, and Happiness. Let's say that the average individual scores about a three on the index, but with a lot of effort and self-improvement a person might develop the qualities allowing him or her to eventually get up to a five. Each individual, of course, has a different set of skills and gifts to work with.
>
> Now imagine a merger (or marriage) where two

The most exciting and powerful marriaging usually brings together two people with different strengths, gifts, and skills.

individuals come together and commit to a partnership that combines all that they are into a new entity. The combined score on the ACH index now averages around six and with work can reach ten. On top of that, a couple's synergy together and their combination and blending of purpose can add an additional five on the index, potentially pushing the score of their oneness up to fifteen.

The oneness reaches an ACH level three times what either could have reached as an individual.

The goal is to create a new oneness that supersedes the old individualness. Creating this can change our lives and lift the level on which we live. But it involves three extraordinarily hard adjustments:

1. Make interdependence your goal instead of independence.
2. Focus on the development of your marriage at least as much as you focus on self-development.
3. Work on making the other half of your partnership happy—rather than your own half.

More on each of these in forthcoming chapters.

2. The Achievement Myth

(AND OTHER MYTHS AND TRUTHS ABOUT PRIORITIES.)

MYTH: Achievements are harder and take more work than relationships.

TRUTH: Relationships are, both in the short-term and the long-term, always more important than achievements; and they are usually harder.

1. **SUB-MYTH: The home supports the career.**

   TRUTH: The career supports the home.

2. **SUB-MYTH: Achievements can be pursued, while relationships just happen.**

   TRUTH: Relationships, particularly the marriage relationship, deserve the most "pursuing" of all; and relationship goals can be as effective as achievement goals.

3. **SUB-MYTH: Parenting is more work than marriaging, and good parents are almost always good marriage partners.**

   TRUTH: Good marriages take constant effort and almost always make for better parenting—but this doesn't necessarily work the other way around.

4. **SUB-MYTH: Marriage is about two individuals, and it works best if the families stay out of it.**

   TRUTH: Your marriage, like it or not, is the joining of two families, so you might as well embrace it. Our in-laws can become our in-loves; the more positive and proactive we are about extended family relationships, the more we will get and the more we will give.

2-1: A'S VERSUS R'S

We love this old cliché: "No one on their deathbed says, 'Oh how I wish I had spent a little more time with the business.'"

The longer we live, the more we realize that relationships are what really matter. Our real legacy is our children, our friends, and—most of all—the marriage we have lived.

Most of us know what our priorities should be, yet the way we live our lives is often so out of sync with what we know matters most. Achievements and accomplishments and accumulation pull at our thoughts, our time, and our energy, leaving too little for our relationships. The A's end up getting prioritized over the R's.

The *things* of our life are somehow more measurable than the *people.* We can set goals for the things, positions, and status we want, but the relationships seem harder and more nuanced, lending themselves less to objectives and deliberate pursuit. How do you set a goal for a relationship? "We'll be 50 percent perfect in five years and 100 percent perfect in ten years"? It just doesn't work as well. Additionally, we get rewards, bonuses, and recognition for accomplishments but not for relationships.

Should the relationships of our lives support our achievements, or should it be the other way around? Do we ask our marriage and our families to bend and flex to accommodate our careers? Or should we view our careers as the support mechanism for our relationships?

Which is the end and which is the means?

It is interesting to think of life in a sort of binary way, being made up of two primary things: achievements and relationships, or A's and R's. Almost everything we do—every ounce of energy we expend, every goal or plan we have—is aimed at one or the other. Both are broad categories.

Achievements can take place at work, in sports or music, in church or community pursuits, and in the everyday tasks of life. Relationships exist with spouse, children, friends, coworkers, neighbors, and even strangers. It is hard to think of anything we do or would want to do that is not some kind of an A or an R.

> **We are generally better at (and better trained for) achievements than relationships.**

Most people, when asked which of the two is more important to them, choose relationships. We tend to think of achievements as things and of relationships as people, and most of us declare that people are more important than things.

Yet when we calculate or keep track of how much time and mental energy we devote to each, we usually get the opposite result. We seem to work harder at achievements than at relationships.

Why is this the case?

Perhaps it is because we are generally better at (and better trained for) achievements than relationships. Very little of our schooling deals with relationships, and at work we are more often measured by our achievements than by our relationships.

We know how to set achievement goals; they lend themselves to time frames, sequencing, percentages, and short-term goals that lead to long-term goals. If I want to make a certain amount of money in ten years, I can figure out what I have to do this year and next year and the year after that, and I can measure exactly how far I still have left to go.

If I want a promotion at work, I can set the goals and make the plans to get what I want. If I want a new car, I can quantify how much it costs and how much I need to save for it or pay on it each month.

But how do we do that goal setting and quantifying with our relationship goals? As mentioned, the "100 percent perfect marriage in ten years, so 10 percent perfect this year" doesn't work very well. How do we quantify and subdivide our R goals? They are simply not the same as A goals!

But that doesn't mean we can't set relationship goals that will work—effective relationship goals can be set and pursued, but we need to go about it in a different way, as explained in the next section.

2-2: SETTING RELATIONSHIP GOALS

Linda: When I married Richard, I thought I was a pretty good goal setter. Little did I know that I was marrying someone who had spent most of his life thinking about goal setting! Before we were married, we started setting one-year, five-year, and ten-year goals. When we got married and were beginning our life in our tiny little student apartment in Boston, I realized that I was a mere baby in the art of goal setting and that Richard was obsessed. He also had a little artistic gene running through his system that made him set goals in unique ways—sometimes putting them on huge foam-core boards or creating goals in pictures rather than in words. When we had our first child in her baby crib with colorful mobiles spinning above her head, it gave Richard the idea to create a giant mobile that hung above our bed with our creatively arranged goals dangling from big wires and strings. It was the first and last thing we saw morning and night. I thought it was cute at the time. Knowing what I know now, I think it was hilarious, consistent, and a perfect illustration of what was to come. As all things do, that grand goal-mobile came down and got discarded when we moved on to our next home. I'd give anything to see it today!

T here are a lot of good ways to set *achievement* goals, but the idea of setting specific *relationship* goals is foreign to most people. Relationships are not measurable or quantifiable like achievements, so we often find it difficult to set clear and specific goals for the improvement of our most important relationships—those with our spouse, children, parents, siblings, and extended family members. We want better relationships, of course, but we usually think of them in general terms rather than trying to set exact goals for the changes we want to bring about.

> Most *achievement* goals are written down with a lot of numbers or percentages. *Relationship* goals require descriptive words instead.

So, most of us end up with a lot of *achievement* goals and not many *relationship* goals.

But consider this fact: A goal is nothing more or less than a clear picture of something specific you want at a precise future moment. Desiring to accomplish or achieve something lends itself to goal-centered thinking because we can imagine a job well done, a promotion received, a salary or pay level obtained, or a running time achieved. We can quantify and segment an achievement and set short-range goals that lead us progressively toward it.

Here is the point: We can do exactly that same kind of visualizing with a relationship. It just takes a more *qualitative* type of thinking and the courage and effort to write a description of the relationship you want with a particular person five years from today.

Most *achievement* goals are written down with a lot of numbers or percentages. *Relationship* goals require descriptive words instead.

The actual exercise is fairly simple. Pick out a person you love and with whom you want to improve your relationship. This could be your spouse, your child, a parent, or just a friend.

Now try to imagine yourself with that person five years from today. Think about how old you each will be and where you might be located.

Focus on really seeing your future selves and on watching, on the monitor of your mind, how you will look, how you will speak to and listen to each other, how you will feel together, how you will communicate with and respond to each other. Have a little vision of the ideal—of how you want it to be. Write a one- or two-paragraph description of what your imagination sees.

Relationship goals take imagination, so kids are often better at setting them than adults. One mom who tried doing relationship goals with her two kids found that they had an easier time than she did. The three of them sat down on a Sunday afternoon earlier this year, and each tried to write down a "relationship goal" for the other two.

The nine-year-old girl wrote this about her vision of her future relationship with her brother:

> It is 2023, and I am fourteen. My brother is sixteen. He can drive now and he drives me to school. We enjoy being together because I am good at telling him what girls think. He looks after me. We tell each other everything and we trust each other. He helps me decide what classes to take and I help him with his math because I am better at it than he is. We are each other's best friend.

Whether these relationship descriptions ever come fully true or not, they can have a guiding influence on how kids view each other and communicate with each other (and with their parents).

When we, as adults, take an attempt at relationship goals, the expansion of thinking that occurs is quite remarkable. To do it, just sit down with a pad of paper, or at the computer, and let it flow. If you are a parent, try to describe the relationship you would like to have with a child five years from today.

Try to imagine your six-year-old at eleven and visualize the relationship you want to have at that point. Describe it on paper. Use that imagination!

Don't worry about the quality of your writing—no one is going to see this but you. And don't worry about setting your expectations too high and then having those hopes dashed if the future doesn't turn out quite like you described it. Just remember that by thinking about a relationship in its future tense, you can impact that relationship in positive ways.

And by thinking about the family relationships you want to have in five years, you begin to understand things that you must start doing today to begin to bring that goal, that *relationship*, to pass.

Of course, the most important relationship goals will be with your spouse, so these are ones to take the most time on and to put the most mental effort into. Write your vision of your relationship in five years in as much detail as you can imagine. Be realistic but idealistic. Try to envision the picture you create in words and to think about it as real—at least in its potential. Setting this kind of a relationship goal with a spouse is one of the most meaningful acts of marriaging that we have ever observed (or practiced).

And yes, there were two little five-year-out relationship descriptions dangling and spinning from that goal-mobile hanging above our bed all those years ago.

Over time, as you consider and add to your future marital relationship description and ponder it regularly, you will notice that your present reality and that future reality are gradually coming closer together.

And remember, any time we spend thinking about and developing relationships, particularly with our family—and most importantly with our spouse—is time well spent.

Because nothing matters more.

2-3: MARRIAGING

When we introduced this new word to a parenting class we teach—a class full of bright young moms and dads—we asked the class how many thought they worked harder at parenting than at marriaging. We were not surprised to see that 90 percent of the parents raised their hands.

Then we asked them if they thought this was a problem. There was some hesitation, but people started to realize that, yes, it is a problem because the marriage relationship should come first.

The old nursery rhyme got it right:
"First comes love, then comes marriage,
Then comes the baby in the baby carriage."

This is not only the right sequence, it is the right priority. Because, here is the thing:

Strong marriages always stimulate better parenting, but strong parenting does not always stimulate better marriages.

This can be a problem, because so many couples today work harder on their parenting than they do on their marriaging.

It's a question of prioritizing both marriaging and parenting but realizing that the former actually comes first and has more influence on the latter than the latter has on the former.

Linda: When we had our ninth child, I clearly remember being overwhelmed as I cuddled that little baby in my arms at the hospital and said to Richard, "Okay, honey, we now have nine children. I can't have ten children. You have got to take care of yourself!

Yikes! That was wrong! Even though I was clearly worried about spending time with each of the kids and may not have had the capacity for "equal time" with Richard, I needed to realize that, through deliberate thought, my priority was still him and not them. Of course, there were times when we both had to admit that we were just in survival mode and trying to endure the mayhem. But through it all we both tried to remember that the most important relationships in our lives were with each other.

Parenting is a real, active word that implies learning and becoming better; in fact, it has risen to become an art and a science and is a huge category on Amazon. *Marriaging*, on the other hand, is a made-up word because we don't have the same active, involving, thinking word surrounding the marriage relationship—a word that can be used as a proactive verb that describes our quest to improve at the most important relationship in our lives.

We should be thinking longer and harder about marriaging than about anything else. Because how well we do at marriaging will affect our head, heart, health, and happiness more than anything else.

It's like that announcement the flight attendant makes on every flight: "If the oxygen masks drop down, put one on yourself first, and then on your children." If we take care of our marriages first, we will be in better shape to raise our children. There are clear connections between how good people do in their marriage relationships and how good they are at parenting.

"A father who has a good relationship with the mother of his children is more likely to be involved and to spend time with his children and to have children who are psychologically and emotionally healthier," says W. Bradford Wilcox, director of the National Marriage Project at the University of Virginia and one of that study's authors. "Indeed, the quality of the marriage relationship affects the parenting behavior of both parents."[1]

It seems obvious when you think about it—someone who is good at one relationship is more likely to be good at others. But it is more than that. When a father and mother are in love, at peace with each other, and in sync in how they think about things, they become far more capable, enthusiastic, and involved parents. The security of a good marriage relationship gives parents the confidence and clarity to develop great relationships with their kids.

And parents who are on the same page are obviously more consistent with their children and more in agreement on everything from discipline to motivation.

It is problematic that so many parents are working conscientiously on being good parents but not working with equal diligence and commitment on being good at marriaging. It's like parenting is some defined skill set that people can work on and progress on and constantly try to get better at, while being a husband or wife is just a role that is too often taken for granted and not developed or perfected in any conscious way. That is why we like to use the new action-term, *marriaging.*

When a father and mother are in love, at peace with each other, and in sync in how they think about things, they become far more capable, enthusiastic, and involved parents.

As the wise maxim says: "The best thing a father can do for his children is to love their mother, and the best thing a mom can do for her kids is to love their dad."

Nothing gives children more security than seeing how in love their parents are. If you want to see warm, secure, delighted smiles spread across your children's faces, grab your partner and have a big, long kiss right for all to see!

Of course, there are wonderful, stalwart single parents doing a heroic and effective job of parenting. In some ways, the relationship between a single parent and children is refreshingly simple and straightforward—as that parent and child(ren) are often everything to each other.

But to those fortunate enough to belong to two-parent families, the relationship between those two parents is the most important relationship in the family. Because of this, how hard it is worked on is a huge factor in the well-being of the children, in the happiness of the parents, and in the security felt by all in the household.

And again, the cause and effect arrow points from a good marriage to good parenting—but does not necessarily point the opposite way. Couples who work harder on their parenting than on their marriaging may actually weaken their marital bond.

Prioritize *marriaging*, and your *parenting* will get better!

Prioritize your *marriage*, and your *life* will get better!

2-4: SEEING THE LONG VIEW (AND THE INCOMPARABLE VALUE) OF THE HIGHEST PRIORITY

All marriages go through their ups and downs, and we have become convinced that staying married and strengthening our marriage over time are often a matter of realizing just how high the stakes are. We are committed enough that we fight our way through the tough times with never even a thought of giving up or throwing in the towel.

Let us try a metaphor that may be helpful in grasping how much is at stake and in giving us all the long-range perspective that may get us through the rough patches that every marriage experiences.

Imagine that you have started a business. Imagine that you put everything you have into this new company—all your money and all your borrowing power—and committed yourself to make that business work.

There are some good years and some bad years. Now you have had the company for some time, and in some ways you are getting a little tired of it. And there are problems! You get audited by the IRS and have to pay some back taxes that you can't afford. One of your employees has been embezzling from you and it is putting a strain on everything. And sometimes you feel that you don't even really like the product you are producing, and you find the day-to-day process of running the business somewhat tedious and even boring.

You keep reminding yourself how much you have invested in the company—both in money and in time—and so you keep at it, slogging away and doing your best. But it just seems like things aren't getting any easier, and more and more often you have the feeling that you should just get out—sell the company and start over. Maybe you could build a better business the next time around, one you would enjoy more and that would produce a better product.

But then something happens. You have a vision one day of what the company could be worth if you held onto it and kept it going. This little epiphany overwhelms you and you fully and deeply believe that if you persevere and give it your all, the company will one day be worth not a million dollars, not even one hundred million, but one billion dollars!

Now, armed not only with the motivation of all that you have put into the business, but with the unimaginable amount that it will one day be worth, you deepen your commitment and give all you have to making it succeed.

The business, of course, is metaphorical for our marriages; for all we put into them, for the problems and doubts and challenges we feel, for the tendencies we sometimes have to want to give up or to start over with someone else, and for the inestimably huge worth that a marriage will eventually have if it endures and lasts forever. The product and the other officers and employees of the company represent our children and the motivation of sticking with it and sticking together.

The benefits of getting through the tough times—of never giving up, of prioritizing your marriaging above everything else—are incalculable. That marriage can one day be more valuable to you

Keeping the long-range benefits in mind will help you struggle through all the challenges along the way.

than a one-billion-dollar company. It can become the single greatest blessing and possession of your life. In the years ahead, you can have the joy and security of gowing old together, of marveling at your posterity, and of never knowing lonliness and despair that would otherwise overtake you.

Keeping the long-range benefits in mind will help you struggle through all the challenges along the way. Draw from this analogy and find the motivation you need to make your marriage commitments absolutely firm and to maximize and prioritize your constant efforts to strengthen and improve this most important and highest potential asset of your life.

This metaphor could also include a caveat: If the company was producing toxic waste and abusing people, it would not be worth preserving.

2-5: REMEMBER AND ANTICIPATE THE STAGES OR PHASES OF MARRIAGE

Pondering the past and anticipating the future can give both perspective and motivation to the present.

As we think of our marriages as permanent and durable, we can try to get in the habit of viewing our union in the past, the present, and the future. Each stage of marriage can bring its own unique joy and a growing dimension of communication and compatibility. And as we learn to think about the whole sweep, the little blips or blowups along the way seem rather small and inconsequential.

Give a little thought—and it can be a very pleasant thought—to the earlier stages of your marriage; and do a little positive anticipation of your future stages.

One of the advantages of waiting fifty years to write a marriage book is that all of the phases, for us, are in our rear-view mirror. But one of the drawbacks is that we may have forgotten quite a lot. Right?

Well, surprisingly, you forget less than you might think. Something about the key relationship of life has a memory preserving quality about it. Recollecting and anticipating together is both enjoyable and instructive. Reflect with us on phases you have finished and dream a little about the ones still to come. We also encourage you to do a little evaluation of your own balance between *relationships* and *achievements* in each state. Use this as an exercise to continue your improvement in prioritizing the things that matter most.

FIRST PHASE: YOUNG MARRIEDS WITHOUT CHILDREN

COMBINING CULTURES AND STARTING YOUR OWN.

Lately, it's been easier to remember what is was like in those budding, early days of our marriage as we have watched our first grandson and his delightful fiancée approach their wedding day. Even as we write, they are within a month of their marriage—they are so young and so much in love! They make us laugh with their delight in each other and the naivety of what lies in store! Luckily, they come from similar cultures and seem to be a perfect match. Even though they are uncertain about the details of their lives as a married couple, they are determined to work their way through their college years together. She will be working two jobs on the side and he essentially working a full-time job on the varsity volleyball team. They are giddy about starting their life together (and hopefully also gritty).

> ***Linda:*** *When we were married, Richard and I were a little older than our grandson and his fiancée are, having both graduated from college before we began life together. But we were pretty oblivious to what was ahead as well. After our*

*marriage and a four-day honeymoon at a friend's cabin at
Bear Lake (which, unbeknownst to us, would become the
vicinity of our future family gathering place), we headed for
Boston. I had a job teaching music at a junior high school
near Boston, and Richard was plunging into the intense world
of his first year at the Harvard Business School. I managed
to prepare lesson plans while he prepared his WACs (Written
Analysis of Case studies). I found my way to the grocery store
and then cooked meals for six every day—I ate one portion
and he ate the other five. He was a tall, lanky, eating machine
with a magnificent metabolism.*

We created relationships with lifelong friends during the years
we were in Boston and collected precious memories, including
watching Richard walk home from school across the solid ice on the
Charles River from our twenty-second-floor student-housing balcony. Since we had basically no money—along with many friends in
the same boat—our favorite entertainment was seeing who could get
paper airplanes to fly the farthest across the river from our balcony.

The two of us spent a fair amount of time "combining our cultures" with some angst. Even though our backgrounds were similar,
our ideas of how, when, and why to do things were not. Luckily, we
were totally committed to each other and, looking back, I think we
quite enjoyed our arguments. We thought life was so grueling and
complicated!

Although we knew that our main job was taking care of each
other, the demands at the business school and preparations for
teaching my seventh-grade kids swept us down the river toward
the exhausting job of accomplishing achievements. And that ever-
present need to achieve sometimes rocked the ship!

SECOND PHASE:
MARRIED WITH YOUNG CHILDREN

IN THE THICK OF IT.

> *Linda: I call this phase of marriaging the "in the trenches" era. We were both committed to a large family from the beginning; Richard jokes that I wanted ten children and he wanted two so we compromised at nine. That is funny but not true! We both loved the idea of a large family. Every eighteen months to two years, another child joined us "trailing clouds of glory" and welcomed with jubilation. Our oldest was twelve when our sixth baby arrived—and then three more joined the fun! It's not a path we would suggest for everyone, but we had the space, time, and interest, so we kept on going. We were also writing parenting books by the time the later kids came, and we "needed new material."*

During our early marriaging, Richard was a partner in a demanding management and political consulting company that required his being away from home a lot, sometimes four days a week. He was running political campaigns across the country and in Puerto Rico, and there is no way to escape the fact that career achievements were important in this phase of life and that, to a degree, relationships were suffering.

Within a few years we were getting our kids to twenty-three lessons every week. There were piano, harp, flute, cello, and violin lessons along with three soccer teams—each with two practices and a game every week—and basketball games coming out our ears. On Saturdays, we sometimes sat on gym benches or soccer sidelines all day with a dash to a fast food place for something to munch on while we watched. Homework, science projects, school plays, and orchestra performances all kept us moving every minute of every day. We tried to notice the few moments of joy that poked through now and then to momentarily distract us from our ambition and work goals.

> We wish we had prioritized a little better and done more to enjoy our own relationship and our relationships with each of the kids.

There was always someone who had a problem with a friend. There was always a need to build up an insecure daughter or work with a son with a learning disability. Of course, we were working to maintain our relationships with each other, but we were definitely working harder on our parenting than we were on our marriaging. We still loved each other, but we were mostly just treading our relationship water. Our Sunday Sessions (as explained in Chapter 1-3) were our salvation during those lots-of-fun-but-pretty-chaotic years!

Looking back, we wish we had prioritized a little better and done more to enjoy our own relationship and our relationships with each of the kids.

THIRD PHASE: MARRIED WITH TEENAGERS

THE PHASE YOU DREAD MAY TURN OUT TO BE YOUR FAVORITE.

As we were about to enter life with teenagers (while still having a gaggle of younger kids) we braced ourselves for those infamous, dreaded, horrendous experiences with teens. Luckily (and we do mean luckily because kids "are who they are"), most of the things we feared did not happen! And then the things we never thought of . . . did!

Linda: *I always knew that I loved babies and adored little kids. But believe it or not, I think the teenage years were my favorites. Not during the time that our sixteen-year-old daughter with a brand-new driver's license had two car accidents in one week. Not on the day that we happened to drive past our high school parking lot just in time to see our big van being driven by one of our daughter's friends with a kid "surfing" on the top. Not on the days when we worried about one of the kids not having the right friends or struggling with grades. And definitely not on the days when we all stressed out about preparing for the ACT and SAT tests.*

But the fun was endless as we went to school basketball and football games, enjoyed hordes of kids at our house on Friday nights, and watched our creative children formulate adult ideas and be able to discuss them thoughtfully and clearly. It was inspiring to hear them sing in choirs and small groups and exhilarating to see them win debate tournaments or basketball games and to excel in subjects they loved because of an excellent teacher.

The balance of keeping our marriaging relationship solid while building a steady reliable relationship with our teenagers—who could sometimes be difficult—was like a juggling act; often we dropped the ball. Our commitment to each other, even though there were many disagreements about how to help our teenagers "achieve" success in their endeavors, helped our relationship survive.

FOURTH PHASE: MARRIED WITH GROWN CHILDREN LEAVING HOME

GETTING THEM (AND YOURSELF) READY.

Linda: *This phase lasted longer for us than it will for most of you. Richard and I figure that we had children in grade school (elementary, junior high, or high school) for about thirty years. Then there was another decade or two with some or all of them in college. When our oldest child left home for her first university year, we still had eight children at home; when our first marriage occurred, we still had three children at home.*

There are so many different scenarios during this phase determined by the size and circumstances of your own family, but many of the emotions are the same. As we sent kids off to college, to be missionaries for our church, to study abroad programs, and to new jobs, we realized that sending kids off to the world is different for each phase you are in. When our oldest daughter Saren went off to Wellesley College in Boston, just after she turned eighteen, I spent a lot of time worrying about her—about how she might be doing, adjusting, and feeling. Since she and I both love art, I stocked up on art post cards and stamps and sent her a post card every day for the first year. In doctor's offices, waiting to pick up kids from school, during concerts, and any time I had a spare moment, I was busy writing to keep her afloat. As it turned out she was "doing just fine, thank you!" But she did display the cards and loved my efforts. We had a lovely relationship!

By the time we sent our ninth child, Charity, off to Wellesley, we had accumulated a lot of experience sending off kids. We had learned that by then we had pretty well done our parenting work and, though they would have their ups and downs, they would (aside from the occasional, inevitable crisis) mostly do well and thrive. To be honest, I was tired by that point and looked forward to my new life. Actually, with Charity's strong personality we were more worried about Wellesley than about her. I waved a fond farewell and then went back home with a mixture of anxiety and exhilaration!

Getting ready to send kids off to their new lives is a mental exercise that is important. It's critical to discuss with them, as a couple, not only finances but the issues of taking care of themselves, staying safe, and being true to who they are. As each child leaves, theoretically, there should be more time for your marriage. But somehow it doesn't happen unless you plan it. Keep your goals and achievements in mind and your enduring and exciting new marital relationship as the central goal.

FIFTH PHASE: MARRIED WITH AN EMPTY NEST

AUTUMN IS THE RICHEST TIME.

SIXTH PHASE: MARRIED AND AGING

MANAGING THE TRADE-OFFS.

Since we are now in these last two phases, and since anticipation can be a motivation for us all, they deserve their own separate chapter—which starts on the next page.

2-6: ANTICIPATING THAT FIFTH AND SIXTH STAGE

(PARTLY FOR THE SAKE OF RECOMMITTING OURSELVES TO GETTING THERE.)

As exciting as the spring and summer of your marriage may have been, the full richness of autumn may be the best of all.

The time that the last child leaves the home is often a tough time for marriage partners. The marital relationship in an empty nest takes on a different chemistry and presents different challenges. With no one left to take care of but each other, it can be a wonderful and revitalizing time for marriaging, but without any plan, it can also be a time of real strain. Issues that were tabled or buried while the kids took up the attention and energy can re-emerge as bigger concerns.

Our observation is that couples who simply react to this new time of life do not do nearly as well as couples who are proactive and deliberate about planning what their life together will be like.

It is ironic that many of us plan so carefully for every other aspect of our upcoming retirement but think and plan so little for what has the most importance and is the key to our happiness—the quality and durability of our marriages.

As the empty-nest time approaches, or if it has already arrived, it is wise to do some solid conceptual planning about this new phase of married life. In our case, even as we dreaded the day our last one would leave, we relished and looked forward to having the opportunity to do things that weren't possible (or at least not practical) while the kids were with us. These ranged from simple things like more reading to complex things like more travel and humanitarian service.

It's best not to leave these visions and dreams to chance or generalities. Sit down or take a trip together and make some conceptual plans about what you want to do as a couple after the kids are gone. Give yourself some things to look forward to in order to balance and counteract the dread you may feel about your children leaving. Learn to see the empty nest phase as a natural progression and a great opportunity.*

One couple we know anticipated their empty-nest phase with some apprehension. They had seen other couples pull apart after their kids were gone, so they put a little plan in place. The first thing they did after their last child left was go away together themselves—on a two-week second honeymoon in the Caribbean. It was a relaxed, peaceful time to get to know each other again—not as a mother and a father, but as partners and lovers.

Give yourself some things to look forward to in order to balance and counteract the dread you may feel about your children leaving.

They talked a lot about each other's needs and actually avoided talking about their kids. (They'd done plenty of that in the immediate weeks before.) They made new commitments to each other and

---

*For more on empty-nest marriaging, see the Eyres' earlier book, *Life in Full: Maximizing Your Longevity and Legacy* *took the time to really talk about their life as a couple, both in the past and in the future. They made plans about things they would do together and how they would spend their time. They talked about their biggest hopes and fears entering this new phase of life and decided to be patient with each other and to acknowledge that it would take a little time to make this adjustment.*

Another couple did something similar but in a very different way. They didn't go away together on a big expensive trip, they just talked and hung out together over the course of several evenings just after their last child left for college. They worked at formulating a new plan in a very organized and systematic way, and while the discipline and structure of it might not appeal to all of us, their approach is certainly thought-provoking.

Take the time to reflect and anticipate. Consider getting away together as a couple to think through any or all of these six phases. This is a time to evaluate, both for the past and the future, how well you have done and will do on prioritizing relationships above achievements and balancing the two well enough that neither suffers.

And think about the last phase too. There is something enormously appealing about growing old together, and thinking about it before it happens will be helpful in maximizing the joys and minimizing (or dealing well with) the trials.

2-7: THINKING ABOUT EXTENDED FAMILY RELATIONSHIPS

We tend to think of marriage as being between two individuals. But in fact, marriage is a transition from individualism to collectivism, and it is a merger of two families—a merger we should accept and make the best of.

Most Americans react negatively to the idea of an arranged marriage. The thought creates a mental picture of a young couple forced to wed by controlling families. Most of us cling to the Western idea that we should magically find and fall in love with a soul mate without help or interference from anyone else.

But much of the world disagrees. In many places, marriage is perceived as the merging of two families, and input from many, particularly the parents, is very important and valued. The idea is that if your families like each other and you have similar beliefs, expectations, economic conditions, and aspirations, your marriage has a better chance. And there is an acknowledgment that loving parents may actually know quite a bit about what their own children might need and want to make them happy.

Sound weird?

Maybe we shouldn't judge too fast. Both the highest marriage rates and the lowest divorce rates happen to be in countries where arranged marriage is the norm. This is due in part to the social stigma of divorce, but most would agree that compatible beliefs, families that get along, and similar family cultures are positive factors in a marriage.

And the process certainly doesn't exclude love or choice. The way arranged marriage works among educated people in India, the Middle East, and other places we have observed is that the families (mainly the parents) communicate a lot about their marriage-age children. When two sets of parents agree that their children might be a good match, they have a big party where the young man and the young woman meet formally and where the possibility is celebrated. Then the two young people have some time to communicate, to have a courtship, and to decide whether they want to move forward with the relationship—and ultimately the marriage—or if they prefer to veto the idea and have their parents keep looking.

> *One of the most charming and successful couples we have met in recent years is from Saudi Arabia. They told us how their parents went through this process, how they dated for several months, and how he wanted to marry but she did not. She went off to the United States for graduate school, and his family kept looking. When she came home three years later, however, the two got reacquainted and this time they clicked. They are now happily married, have three wonderful kids, and the two families are best friends.*

Time and again in our travels and speaking in countries where our audiences are mostly from arranged marriages, we ask couples if they liked having their marriage arranged or if they wish their parents had stayed out of it. And we ask if they plan to continue the practice with their own children. These are smart, educated people, successful in their professions and widely traveled. Almost unanimously, they favor the idea of arranged marriage and plan to practice it with their own children.

A marriage, whether we like it or not, is a joining of two families.

So, are we really advocating a system of arranged marriage? No. But what we are suggesting is that young people and whole families would be well served by a mentality where parents are more pro-active in the "looking" process, where their help and suggestions are welcomed by their children, where finding possibilities for a potential marriage is an actual goal within the whole family, and where marriage is viewed as the joining of two entire families.

The real lesson of successful arranged marriages is simply this: A marriage, whether we like it or not, is a joining of two families; the more we can do to become and stay close to the parents, siblings, and family of our spouse, the more fulfillment and joy will come from this greater union.

Reach out more. Think of your spouse's family as your own second family. Put siblings-in-law in an even higher-priority category than friends. Understand that the parents of your spouse are or will be the co-grandparents of your children. Accept the true adage that "blood is thicker than water" and that the better you cultivate and take care of extended and in-law family relationships, the more fulfilling and joy producing they will be as the years go by.

Think of your "in-laws" as your "in-loves."

And remember one more thing: Your children will be (or are) the grandchildren of both of your sets of parents. Nothing has more potential of creating positive, prideful relationships than co-grandparenting, and few things benefit a child more than having two sets of compatible grandparents.*

---

*If you are a grandparent, read more in Linda's book *Grandmothering* or Richard's *Being a Proactive Grandfather.*

3. The Independence Myth

(AND OTHER MYTHS AND TRUTHS ABOUT FREEDOM.)

MYTH: It is best for each spouse to maintain his or her own independence and form a self-reliant two-way partnership.

TRUTH: Independence is overrated and lonely; and it gets more so the longer we live. Interdependence is the acknowledgment of this simple, vulnerable truth and it is a joy to willingly, enthusiastically trade your independence for interdependence. Ultimately, a three-way partnership that recognizes dependence on God is the strongest of all.

1. SUB-MYTH: The key to a good marriage is for both partners to go 50 percent and meet in the middle.

   TRUTH: You may sometimes have to go 90 percent to meet your spouse's 10 percent, and your partner may have to go 90 percent to meet you at other times.

2. SUB-MYTH: Freedom and responsibility are opposites.

   TRUTH: Responsibility and sacrifice for those you love leads to a higher freedom from the "dungeon of self."

3. SUB-MYTH: Needing marriage therapy is a weakness.

   TRUTH: Getting professional help when you need it is always a strength.

3-1: A HIGHER KIND OF FREEDOM

Linda: As a college student, I was fiercely determined to protect my freedom, independence, and options. I wanted to travel the world and I wanted to explore. I wanted marriage at some point, but not until I had proved my independence in numerous ways. When Richard came along and spoiled that, I think I resented it a bit on some levels, but before long we both realized that the new freedoms that came with interdependence were far more liberating than the old freedoms that went with independence.

Little did I know that in time I would be traveling to over seventy countries of the world with him—often with a gaggle of children in tow. Besides explorations to wild and crazy places with the kids, we'd be speaking to parents and families about how important their work is and using our experiences with both successes and failures while raising our own family to help others sort out their own priorities and interdependence.

ndependence and *freedom* are the hallmarks of our American culture and economy and perhaps the best measurements of government and society around the world.

But they are not always so good for marriage.

Committed relationships seem to demand that we willingly give up a portion of our independence and freedom in return for something better. We have to sacrifice some of the quantity of our options for the highest quality option of committed marriage.

The French have a phrase that means, in essence, "it's easy to do stuff on your own and for yourself—the challenge and the joy is doing them with and for others."

Freedom and commitment can, at times, be in conflict with each other.

More than two hundred years ago, Alexis de Tocqueville, a French diplomat, predicted that excessive freedom in America would negatively affect marriages and families.

We willingly give up a portion of our independence and freedom in return for something better.

Much more recently, David Brooks expressed a similar sentiment in the *New York Times*: "People are not better off when they are given maximum personal freedom to do what they want. They're better off when they are enshrouded in commitments that transcend personal choice—commitments to family, God, craft, and country."[1]

Those who are consumed with maximizing their personal freedom, with keeping all of their options open for as long as possible, and with maintaining their independence no matter what are going to have a hard time with the sacrifices and the responsibilities of marriage.

The best way to think about marriage is not in terms of the surrendering or giving up of independence but more as the trading of unfettered freedom for something much better. The something-better is the kind of beautiful *interdependence* that is possible only with someone you love more than yourself. And that kind of love can lead to a self-realization that is more joyful, more peaceful, and more lasting than any form of independence could ever be; and it can open up a whole new kind of freedom that is ultimately more liberating than unlimited personal options.

A great and recurring theme of literature—both sacred and secular—is the idea of "finding yourself by losing yourself" and "overcoming yourself" by loving someone more than yourself. This idea brings with it a whole new level of freedom from selfishness and from preoccupation with one's own needs. George McDonald said, "The love of our neighbor is the only door out of the dungeon of self," and the same would apply, only more so, to the love of spouse and children.[2]

This kind of selflessness and self-discovery requires sacrifice, certainly, but then some form of sacrifice or loss comes to everyone at some point, either voluntary or mandatory. Therefore you might as well choose your personal version early by making the love-sacrifices and commitments of marriage and children. It is never easy, but the sacrifices made by and through caring deeply for others are far better than those that would come later when (and because) you are old and alone.

And the great blessing of choosing to put your own wants in subjection to the needs of loved ones is that later on, when you look back over your life, you will find that the times when you thought you were sacrificing the most were actually the most joyous periods of your life.

3-2: THE CULT OF THE INDIVIDUAL AND THE TRUTH OF "WE OVER ME"

We owe a lot to marriage, and perhaps its greatest blessing is that it keeps us from thinking about ourselves all the time.

We are fascinated that each annual update of the *Oxford English Dictionary* chooses a "word of the year," as determined by a vote of independent linguists. This is the word that, by its common and popular use, best defines where our culture is going. The word of the year for 2013 was *selfie*. This choice symbolized a society that was overemphasizing the importance of the individual self and undervaluing the importance of the family and community. Since then, "selfie" has become not only a word but a way of life.

"Preserving my individual options" seems to be the goal of so many. We hear more and more members of the millennial generation saying things like "marriage would tie me down" or "having kids would really limit my flexibility and my freedom."

The problem is that when we think only of our own options, our own freedom, and our own individual rights, we end up not thinking enough about the needs of other people and about our commitments to our spouse, children, church, neighborhood, and community. Sometimes, being loyal to the people and the institutions we love means intentionally and purposefully giving up some of our personal options.

Most free societies are built around individual rights and personal freedoms, and it sounds almost revolutionary—or even socialistic or communistic—to limit them. Perhaps what is needed is not limits, but balance.

> There are trade-offs between the "freedoms" and options of the individual and the commitment, sacrifice, and responsibility of having a family.

It is not the individual that is the basic unit of society, it is the family. And there are, and always will be, trade-offs between the freedoms and options of the individual and the commitment, sacrifice, and responsibility of having a family.

We must realize that it is the latter, not the former, that creates a strong society and molds individual character. The idea of not wanting to give up personal options and happiness by making commitments or taking on the responsibility and sacrifices of marriage and children is a completely misplaced notion. It is those very sacrifices and commitments that lead to the deepest kind of happiness.

Still, we live in a world that worships the cult of the individual. Everyone wants to be "their own man" or "their own independent woman," and we are sold the bill of goods that therein lies fulfillment.

In actuality though, a constant quest for unfettered freedom and the avoidance of being "tied down" grows increasingly hollow and ever less fulfilling, while commitment and loyalty to people that we love more than ourselves (spouse and children) deepens both how we feel and who we are.

People who have had a bad family experience or who have not had good family examples become part of the demise of the family simply by choosing not to participate in a family life of their own. They decide, based on the false advertising and misleading media of the culture of the individual, to simply abdicate family—to either not have one at all or to not be fully committed to whatever family they have. They begin "looking out for number one" at the expense of the commitments they might otherwise make to those they love.

Perhaps what we all need to remember is this little (and true) cliché: "Those who are all wrapped up in themselves make a very small package."

3-3: WHAT IF . . .

Instead of taking our spouse for granted, we need to think of him or her as the key to who we are, and to value our collective identity more than our individual identities. What if we did that? What difference would it make?

Even as our world becomes more connected electronically, it is becoming less connected emotionally. Whereas it was once nearly impossible to live alone and independent from others, people do it all the time now, and the social and psychological costs are immense.

Human beings, particularly children, need and crave an identity larger than themselves. Unfortunately, if family does not provide it, they will find it other places—possibly in a gang, an online chat room, or group computer game. Our children are part of so many cultures—from the internet culture to the peer culture to the celebrity culture—but when there is no core family culture, they are like atoms without a nucleus.

Many years ago, we created a preschool curriculum for a parent-participation "Joy School"* that has now been used by more than 300,000 families. It teaches twelve "joys" that children can grasp, practice, and feel. The two most popular joys

*See JoySchools.com

are "The Joy of Individual Confidence and Uniqueness" and
"The Joy of Family Security and Identity." Finding a balance
between these two great joys should be the core goal of parents
and marriage partners everywhere.

As great as the sacrifices of parenting are, sacrifices made in the commitment and interdependence of marriage may be even larger. These are the most beautiful and joyful kinds of sacrifice that exist anywhere—where we willingly give up or deprioritize some of our own wants, options, and freedoms in order to look out for and apply our time, efforts, and emotions to the needs of those we love more than ourselves.

Again, we live in an age and a place where individual rights are almost worshiped. Our legal system is designed to protect those rights, and our culture makes heroes of those who are "true to themselves" or who "live their personal dream"—even when they go to the extreme and begin to damage relationships or hurt those they love.

There are many examples of spouses "who finally do something for themselves" by having an affair or leaving a spouse and children for someone who "fulfills them" or who "gives them space and respects their need to find a deeper reality." We have heard of many examples of spouses and parents who felt that the only way they could be brave or "true to themselves" was by leaving their marriage and family for a partner with whom they felt they could "find their true identity."

> **The sacrifices made in a marriage are the most beautiful and joyful kinds of sacrifice that exist anywhere.**

Before any of us go too far down that "individual" path, perhaps we should ask ourselves some "what if" questions (all of them are debatable, but all are worth thinking about):

- What if happiness has more to do with considering the needs of one's spouse and family than with fulfilling one's self?
- What if commitment and fidelity are what allow people to grow more in love over time?
- What if a man is not a perfectible entity, nor a woman, but a married couple is?
- What if there is something to the idea that the yin and the yang are two necessary parts of one whole?
- What if you actually have more power to influence the happiness of your spouse than that of yourself? And what if he or she has more power to influence your happiness than you do?
- What if hanging in there, getting help, and trying harder were a better strategy than "cut and run"?
- What if an addiction to pornography or to online gaming is substituting artificial, cyber satisfaction for the real satisfactions in life?
- What if a more complete re-commitment could actually simplify, de-stress, and shore up a marriage you thought was beyond repair?
- What if prayer together could actually change your hearts?
- What if you really did fall in love with each other once and could do it again?
- What if what you do with your life together is more important than what you do individually?

None of this is to say that marriage is the only way to live or that single individuals cannot accomplish and contribute in powerful and marvelous ways. What we are trying to say is that maybe those of us who are married could value it more; perhaps we would even get better results by prioritizing the union and the spouse more than the self.

3-4: IN PRAISE OF INTERDEPENDENCE

We sometimes start off our lectures with the question, "Would you trade your independence for interdependence?" Most people say "no!" Their first instinct is that they don't want to trade their independence for anything, particularly for something as weak and self-diminishing as interdependence, which is often associated with codependence.

We live in a world where independence is the perceived goal of almost everything. We are conditioned to want financial independence as well as mental and emotional independence. We see any type of dependence on someone else as a weakness, and we find it much easier to say "I love you" than "I need you."

Many also think the alternative to independence is *codependence*, which Google defines as "excessive emotional or psychological reliance on a partner, typically requiring support due to an illness or addiction." And who would want that?

But interdependence is not codependence. It is something much different and much more beautiful. It is a mutual dependence that is chosen in love, and it makes those who choose it more, not less, free.

With many, independence is almost an obsession. Young people today want to avoid being dependent on anyone. But not needing anyone and always relying solely on yourself can become the ultimate recipe for loneliness.

Interdependence is the conscious choice of commitment, the deliberate decision to intertwine your life with the person you love most.

Interdependence is so much better. It is the conscious choice of commitment, the deliberate decision to intertwine your life with the person you love most. It is the sacrifice of something good for something better.

Interdependence is the choice you make when you opt for the bonds of committed matrimony, and there is security, joy, and natural peace within interdependence that independence has never known.

Choosing interdependence moves us along the scale from selfishness to selflessness. It releases us from constant worry about ourselves and admits us to the more service-centered land of worry about others—particularly about the one you love more than yourself.

Ralph Waldo Emerson said, "The mass of men worry themselves into nameless graves, while here and there a great unselfish soul forgets himself into immortality."

That kind of immortality happens largely through acknowledged and accepted interdependence. Someone who is always seeking his own happiness seldom finds it. But someone who is genuinely trying to make his or her spouse happy usually succeeds.

To summarize the case we are making here, we suggest that there are "three S's" that speak for the superiority of interdependence over independence:

SYNERGY.

When interdependence is chosen and committed to in love, you become more than the sum of your parts. The total of what you can accomplish together and what you can feel together is much more than twice what either of you can achieve or experience alone.

SECURITY.

While the natural extension of independence is loneliness and isolation, the reward and result of interdependence is a deep sense of comfort and security. Someone to take care of and someone to take care of you is not an indication of weakness, but an enhancer of happiness.

SOCIETY.

Even though we talk a lot in this country about individual rights and individual freedoms, the basic unit of a strong society and of a strong economy is the household unit—the family. And statistics show time and again that married couples with children not only perpetuate the human race but also produce more, earn more, and contribute more than individuals living alone. Working together and combining resources has challenges, of course, but there are many reasons right up there with love to invest in marriaging.

If you are lucky enough to have someone you love more than yourself, giving up your independence in favor of interdependence may be the best trade you ever make.

3-5: DON'T JUST BE HYDROGEN AND OXYGEN—BE WATER!

Hydrogen, oxygen, and water can be a metaphor for committed marriage.

The reality is that the marriage commitment to interdependence does not lessen you as an individual—it enhances you. You are still you. You have your views and your opinions and your skills and your unique nature as much as you ever did. When approached with love and commitment, marriage can create an almost magical synergy where the total is greater than the sum of its parts.

Hydrogen, by itself, is a gas possessing many unique properties. Oxygen is another gas with its own set of qualities. But when they are combined in a committed, proportioned, fused sort of way, they become marvelous, clear, flowing, life-giving *water*.

Now life is not always easy for water; it can be evaporated, frozen, even dammed. But, oh, what a miracle water is. Water can do things and go places and bring about results that neither hydrogen nor oxygen, by themselves, could even imagine.

The hydrogen is still hydrogen—it has not lost or given up

Marriage can create an almost magical synergy where the total is greater than the sum of its parts.

any of what it is. And the same is true for the oxygen. But by combining, joining, and committing to each other, they have become something more. They have become the magic of water.

And they and the whole world are better off for it.

Linda: There are days when I complain about Richard's idiosyncrasies. I become grumpy when he "surprises" me with yet another new idea that requires some serious re-scheduling; however, I don't know what I would do without Richard's "oxygen" when I need his advice and support. I like to think that I'm like hydrogen. (Maybe more like a hydrogen bomb on some days. It takes quite a lot of stress to create a meltdown in me, but it happens.) When Richard adds his oxygen, which includes reason and logic, I often reject it until I can't resist any longer and the melting together of our two "gases" creates some pretty great water.

My sister lost her husband when they were both fifty-seven. It was a devastating blow! He was diagnosed with stage-four stomach cancer at nine o'clock one morning and he died at one o'clock that afternoon. Thirteen years have passed since then, including lots of hard times with her seven wonderful kids. When her husband passed, all of her children were married; however, as any of you with adult children know, that doesn't mean there are not continuing problems—and a lot of them. She has dealt with her children's divorces; a son with an alcohol addiction; a four-year-old granddaughter with leukemia, a relapse after treatment, and a complete bone marrow transplant; and kids finding jobs and starting new businesses. These are just a few of the challenges that she has had to face alone.

Right after she lost him, my sister was in shock for a while, trying to reorient and reorganize her life. She missed his smile and his sense of humor dearly. But with the passing of time the things that she says she misses most are his help with making decisions, giving advice to the kids, and most of all the support and comfort he always provided during hard times. Even though husbands may have strange habits that drive us crazy, those irritations pale in the light of the pure oxygen they provide, which combines with our hydrogen in trying times to create the life-giving delight of clear, pure water.

3-6: AN INTERDEPENDENCE LESSON FROM ADAM AND EVE

There is something we can learn from the first story of the Bible—from our first parents, Adam and Eve. Whether you think of them literally or as an instructive fable, their story is perfectly relevant to marriages and families today and teaches us a lot about interdependence.

An acquaintance of ours, *New York Times* columnist Bruce Feiler, has written a book intriguingly called *The First Love Story: Adam, Eve, and Us*, which is enlightening on many levels. Feiler sees Eve as the heroine of the story—the one who figured it out and who loves Adam enough to share the fruit with him. He sees the account as a love story with the two protagonists again and again choosing each other and remaining together. They go through every kind of tribulation while sharing their joys and their sorrows and facing together the burdens of overwhelming parenting crises, including the murder of one of their sons by another.

Speaking for ourselves, the most powerful part of this story is that God makes Adam and Eve equal. In fact, he makes them more than equal, he makes them one—he makes them interdependent. Consider the possibility that the word rib *in the Genesis account may be a bit mistranslated. The original Hebrew word* tsela *occurs in many other places in the Bible and translates better as "side" than as "rib," suggesting that Eve and Adam were created side by side as equals—as two individuals who were separate and different but equal, with each needing the other to complete themselves.*[3]

Feiler even takes that possibility a step further—and we are paraphrasing and interpreting now—suggesting that perhaps Adam, the first human, was initially created as both male and female and that God then separated humanity into two complementing parts, a man and a woman, who could come together to partner, procreate, and parent the population of the planet.

Whether the story is taken literally or figuratively, we love the symbolism of "side by side" and of the interdependence that it suggests. Rather than one being taken from the other, both come about as equal parts of one whole, needing each other to be complete and to find their full selves.

So, what is a message of Adam and Eve that married couples perhaps do not think enough about? Simply that love is the most important thing and that our natural and original state was an interdependence that we should strive to regain.

Could a three-way partnership be even better if the third partner is God or the spirit or a higher power? If a three-way partnership were shaped like a triangle, with God at the top corner and the husband and wife at the bottom corners, and if the goal of each spouse was to draw closer to God, would their movement in that direction also draw them ever closer to each other? And could the wonderful quality of interdependence in marriage be even further enhanced by the humble and vulnerable acknowledgment that we are not only interdependent on each other but dependent on a higher power?

4. The Perfection Myth

(AND OTHER MYTHS AND TRUTHS ABOUT HAPPINESS AND EXPECTATIONS.)

MYTH: I can find (or create) a perfect match for myself and then I will be happy.

TRUTH: Some married couples are better matched than others; there are even those who believe they have found their soul mate. But most marriages are about accommodation and adjustment—and more about changing our own minds than about fixing our spouse's.

1. **SUB-MYTH: I can fix my spouse.**

   TRUTH: You can't. And you might not like the result if you did. Better to work harder at changing yourself than at changing your partner.

2. **SUB-MYTH: Your job is to love yourself; and you are responsible for your own happiness, not anyone else's.**

   TRUTH: It is important to accept and love yourself, but caring more about another whom you love more than yourself is the surest way to receive joy as well as to give it.

3. **SUB-MYTH: If you settle (or have settled) for someone who seems less than perfect, you will never be really happy.**

   TRUTH: Marriage is not a game of perfect. It's about adjusting and improving and getting happier by supporting each other.

4. **SUB-MYTH: Your marriage is going to turn out to be pretty much like your parents' marriage.**

   TRUTH: Many who have bad memories of their parents' marriage are motivated by those memories to fashion a very different kind of marriage for themselves.

4-1: "I CAN FIX HIM"

Linda: On that fateful snowy night fifty Februarys ago when Richard totally surprised me with a diamond engagement ring at the top of the Old Main Tower, the central historic old building at Utah State University, I was stunned! I had worries about our relationship. I felt that there were things he needed to change about himself. He was so strong-willed, "out of the box," and flamboyant, and I was a quiet (but driven) rule-keeper. He had even broken the rules to get us to the top of that tower, which had been condemned. He had worked his magic and found a cohort in crime—a night watchman who provided a key and a warning that we needed "to be quick up there."

My whole life passed before me as I watched the snowflakes fall and considered whether or not I could live with this guy forever. After a long wait, a peace came over me and I decided that my deep love for him trumped all of his faults. Not only that, I was really convinced that I could fix him! So I said yes! And though the poor security guard who had provided our secret rendezvous was wringing his hands at the bottom of the stairs for almost an hour as we soaked in the joy of the moment, I gradually realized that it was the best decision of my life!

The years that followed were full of so much fun and joyful happiness, but they were also mixed with dark days and long discussions about things I was not happy about or things that Richard needed to change. It took many years for me to discover that Richard was good at modifying things about himself that he could see troubled me. I began to realize that he was who he was and that I too had some things that I needed to change but probably never would. I learned to relish his uniqueness and support him in his wild adventures. I think I became more adventurous and surprised him with some of my own changes to try to be more like him in the ways that I admired. Slowly and steadily, both of us began making little changes that edged us a little further down the long, impossible road to perfection!

We know a young man who really struggled to find a perfect soul mate. Going through relationship after relationship, he always found something that made his current person of interest not quite right. During one relationship, he decided that it really bothered him when his girlfriend kind of dragged her feet when she walked. He is now in his forties and not yet married (and probably wishing that he had let that and some other little imperfections go). There are so many young adults out there looking for soul mates and perfection. With the perspective of shared values and with real love and genuine appreciation for the uniqueness of our partners, we may find that the things we thought needed to be fixed may in fact be just the things that *we* need most or that make our spouse endearing. Sometimes the very things that

Sometimes the very things that bother us most about a partner are just another version of the things that we love the most.

bother us most about a partner are just another version of the things that we liked most about them when we were falling in love.

On the other hand, making changes within ourselves is one the hardest things we attempt in life. Working to change things that are obvious obstacles to a happy relationship may be the most important work you will ever do.

4-2: THE HARDEST LESSON OF MARRIAGE

Richard: *At one particularly stressful and busy stage of our marriage—I was traveling with business almost constantly and Linda was trying to keep up with her music and string quartet while she managed and taxied five kids all over town—we slipped into an unusually critical-of-each-other period. Without getting into the painful details, let me just say that she pointed out at every opportunity—and there were a lot of them—that I was controlling, manipulative, and couldn't meet her needs. I retaliated with how judgmental and self-righteous and unsupportive she sounded. Those labels started to stick, and, more frighteningly, they started to fit. It was a period when, no matter what else went well, everything felt like failure and frustration because we felt so deeply our dissatisfaction with each other. The hidden blessing in it was that we began to realize how much we needed each other's approval, how much power we had over the other's sense of well-being, and how overwhelmingly important we were to one another.*

t is natural, in a marriage relationship, to think about what you need from your spouse, about what you expected and wanted from your spouse when you married, and to worry about how many of your expectations have come to pass. It's human to be highly conscious of how many of your needs are being met. And with these thoughts come all kinds of feelings about the ways you wish that your spouse would change.

- Why can't he see what I need?
- Why can't she be more like me (or like my mom)?
- Why doesn't he try harder to make me happy?
- Why doesn't she like more of the things I like or at least support me on things I like that she doesn't?
- Why isn't he the soul mate I thought he would be?

Many of us go into marriage thinking we are going to be able to change our spouse into the person we want him or her to be—into the person who will fulfill our needs and give us all the things we want.

When it doesn't happen quite like that, we feel disappointed and even resentful. Some of us do this silently and let the things he does or the things she doesn't do build up inside of us, gradually deepening our resentment and pulling us further and further apart. Others get aggressive in telling their spouse the ways he is letting them down or the things she ought to be doing for them. The suffering in silence can turn us into a moping sad sack; the criticizing and complaining can turn us into a nag.

A true principle of marriage is that our partners gradually start living up to whatever reputation we give them. If they are thought of as

A true principle of marriage is that our partners gradually start living up to whatever reputation we give them.

inconsiderate, they become more so. If we label them as sloppy, they start to fit that image. If we put them in an *impulsive* box, they start to fit in that box. The more they feel that they can't live up to our expectations, the less they try and the more they feel like failures. The more we tell them they are not meeting our needs, the less confident they feel and the more likely they are to keep disappointing us. When we tell our spouse that he or she is not meeting our needs, it becomes proof of failure, and he or she will either push back and fight or withdraw and give up.

The simplest but hardest lesson of marriage is this: Your spouse is not you.

Constant dissatisfaction and criticism, when expressed or even when held in, can emasculate a man and emotionally abuse a woman. The fact is that we actually have more influence and power over our spouse's happiness and well-being than we do over our own, and when we are negative and down on each other we can both spiral down in very dark and difficult ways.

But there is another way!

How about instead of thinking so much about what he isn't doing for you, you start focusing on what you can do for him? How about instead of trying to make her into what you thought you wanted her to be, you start focusing on helping her become the best of what she really is?

There is a wonderful truth that, when learned and implemented, can inject a wonderful and simple kind of happiness into our marriages. It goes like this: "Strive to understand and focus on your spouse's needs, and gradually—magically—your needs will also be met."

Again, it is so natural to want your spouse to be more like you, to want the same things you want, to like the same things you like, to think the same way you think, and to have the same love language that you do. But in actual fact, as mentioned earlier, few of us would like to be married to a clone of ourselves. It would end up being a little boring and there would be little opportunity for synergy or for learning from each other. Instead, we need to learn to celebrate our differences; love the things about our spouse that are different from us; and support, encourage, and build on the interests, talents, gifts, and strengths that our spouse has.

The simplest but hardest lesson of marriage is this: Your spouse is not you. Your spouse is not your mom or your dad. Your spouse is not the dreamed-up, idealized vision you may have had in your mind. Your spouse is a unique, talented, quirky, potentially wonderful person who is better at a whole host of things than you will ever be; your job is to love that uniqueness, recognize and support those talents, appreciate and love those quirks, and magnify that potential—shifting your focus from trying to make yourself happier by changing her to trying to make *her* happier by changing *yourself.*

Nothing is harder, but nothing is better!

4-3: BE CAREFUL ABOUT WHAT YOU WOULD CHANGE

(AND A LITTLE POETIC ADVICE FOR HUSBANDS.)

Richard: *Each year, I make a feeble effort on Valentine's Day to write a poem to or for or about my sweetheart. (Not that this is something you would or should do—but this particular poem makes a point that fits with the dispelling of this myth.)*

This poem wasn't actually to Linda, but it was about our relationship and it came out of a realization I had a while back, a little aha *moment actually, which I think may have made Linda quite happy on some level. (And I know it made me happier, so it starts with that word.)*

Happy is the man who comes to the epiphany
    That even if he had a magic wand,
    He would not change one single little thing
About his wife . . . .
Real-eyes-ing
That a wife is a very complex
Physical/mental/spiritual organism,
And that tweaking one small part
Might impact or affect related aspects,
And could potentially alter or change
The very things he loves about her most.
Getting this straight in our guy-minds

May allow us to get over the little bugs
And appreciate the whole, complete,
Interrelated and symbiotic package—
Rather than trying to disconnect one little wire somewhere
That might explode the whole essence.
After all, if you re-wrote one tiny word
In one dialogue of a masterful play,
It might change the whole drama.
If you altered one chromosome
It might throw the whole double helix out of kilter
And produce a different animal.
So, we accept the best and worst aspects together,
Under-stand-ing
That they all are parts of one Valentine whole.

If you can learn to do this, to fully accept your spouse, it will pro-vide two gargantuan benefits. First, it will enhance your own calmer, sweeter, deeper happiness. Second, (believe it or not) it will increase the chance that, short or long term, she will, without harming other parts or disrupting the whole organism (as she alone and no one else can), improve the very things you would have ill-advisedly used your magic wand on. This may happen, or maybe it will just seem like it has because, post-epiphany, you won't notice the bugs anymore.

4-4: WHOSE HAPPINESS CAN YOU INFLUENCE?

(AND THE INCALCULABLE BLESSING OF HAVING SOMEONE YOU LOVE MORE THAN YOURSELF.)

Sometimes in our speeches or seminars, we ask married individuals in our audience this same intriguing question: "Whose happiness do you think you have more control over, your spouse's or your own?" People usually jump to the conclusion that you have the most control over your own happiness. But when they really think about it, and when we go through some case studies, most conclude that they have more influence over their partner's sense of well-being than they do over their own.

Let's examine more closely the theme mentioned earlier—the question of whose happiness you have more control over: your own or your partner's.

If you get up tomorrow determined to make yourself happy and then spend the whole day trying to, and then you get up the next day focused entirely on making your spouse happy and spend that whole day working at that goal—on which of the two days will you have the most success?

Start your examination of the question by pondering your partner deeply. Who is your spouse really? What are his or her characteristics? If you could choose ten adjectives to describe your husband or wife at his or her best, what would those words be?

What does your spouse need? If you had that magic wand from the last chapter and wanted to use it for giving rather than for changing, what five things would you give her with a wave of the wand?

Now what if you didn't have the magic wand—could you still give your spouse those five needs?

The sad, simple fact is that someone who is always seeking his own happiness seldom finds it. But the happy counter-fact is that someone who is genuinely trying to make his or her spouse happy usually succeeds. Seeking your own happiness can turn into something resembling narcissism. Seeking your spouse's happiness can turn into a great marriage.

And the married state, when it is approached this way, is the most natural and joyful lifestyle that has ever been discovered.

Of course, there are single people who are happy, who enjoy a full life, and who contribute much to others. Yet most Americans who never have been married say they would like to be at some point in their lives, according to the Pew Research Center.[1] We are wired for interdependence. We instinctively want to be with someone and take care of someone. We are made to love.

And we who are married ought to do our best to appreciate it more. The fact is that having someone you love more than yourself is an incalculable blessing. It changes how we think. It changes how we act. It changes who we are.

Devoting yourself to the happiness of other people is a great and wonderful thing, but devoting yourself to the happiness of one other person—the one you love most—may be the single greatest

The best way, and the simplest way, to forget yourself is by devoting yourself to the happiness of your spouse.

determining factor in most every aspect of your life. This devotion can determine your own day-to-day happiness, the development of your character, where and how you live, and how long you live.

And, of course, it will have the same determining influence on the one you love.

As we quoted earlier, Ralph Waldo Emerson said, "See how the masses of men worry themselves into nameless graves, while here and there a great unselfish soul forgets himself into immortality."

The best way, and the simplest way, to forget yourself is by devoting yourself to the happiness of your spouse. And in our devotion to spouse and our forgetting of self, the happiness we were *not* seeking floods into our own lives.

We have two separate, special friends who illustrate unselfish, unconditional love in a way that is truly dramatic. One is a friend of over forty years who cared devotedly for his first wife through the last fourteen years of her life as she was completely incapacitated with Lou Gehrig's disease. He then married again only to see his second wife develop severe Alzheimer's, and he lovingly cared for her for another ten years until she passed. Now, in his late seventies, he is marrying again. His sacrifices for love have made him into a great, deep, wise soul.

Another friend, an entrepreneur and world traveler, has watched his vivacious wife of four decades rapidly decline with dementia. He still prioritizes her above all else, takes her wherever he can, and treats her with palpable respect and love. When he read an early draft of this book's section on commitment, he said, "When you love someone more than yourself and then dementia comes—or Alzheimer's or an accident that leaves your partner in a coma—hopefully by then the 'end game' is so clear and the relationship foundation so strong, that nothing else matters. Pure love takes over and you figure out a way to make things the best that they can be for your partner, yourself, family, and friends."

4-5: THE FIVE C'S OF HAPPINESS IN MARRIAGE

In our many decades of working with families and observing all kinds of marriage situations, we have become convinced that there are five elements that maximize the chances for a marriage to be nourishing, loving, enduring, and—yes—happy.

A long with knowing what will make each other happy, it is nice to know what makes the two of you collectively happy. As couples, we need to ask ourselves: Are we consistently doing the things that underscore and recognize the happiness we feel in being together and in being committed to one another? What are some of the specific things we can do, the habits we can form, and the attitudes we can adopt that protect the inherent happiness of our relationship?

The problem is that many are losing touch with the most basic things that promote marital well-being and happiness. People are forgetting that there are some ingredients that must be supplied if they want to find a reliable recipe for a romantic, joyful, lasting marriage.

Don't glance at this list and disqualify yourself if you are not observing all of its items, because the lovely thing about these elements is that they can actually be recovered within a relationship even if they have not always been practiced.

None of them are easy though, nor should they be, because they are all part of the hard work that it takes to live happily and romantically with another person for the rest of your life.

We call them the five C's of marital happiness.

The problem is that many are losing touch with the most basic things that promote marital well-being and happiness.

CHASTITY (AND FIDELITY)

The words sound old-fashioned to us today, which is an indication of how far society's expectations have slipped. In a world that has become amoral on many levels, sex is often thought of as a form of recreation rather than a sacred gift that one can choose to share with only one other person. Yet there is no question that those who make that exclusive choice find a higher realm of security and joy.

Nothing is more destructive to marriage than a spouse who finds another sexual relationship. Whether that new relationship is found through casual acquaintances, while traveling, online, or through pornography, it is the hardest thing to overcome in a marriage. But it *can* be overcome. Remember that chastity is not something that is gone forever if you lose it. Chastity can be regained, reclaimed, and then maintained when you realize that it is what you want.

COURTSHIP

Another concept that many seem to think is from a bygone age is real one-on-one dating. Dating can be not only the best way to get to know another person but also a wonderful and exciting kind of wooing (there's another old but quite wonderful word). It can generate the kind of exploring and discovery that exercises both our creativity and our constraint.

The alternatives of hanging out and hooking up have none of the beautifully romantic potential of real courtship. And courtship is not just something that should precede marriage; it should continue and even reach new levels within marriage. Married couples that still try to manage a romantic, weekly date—even if it involves a lot of logistics and babysitters—seem to preserve and even build on the excitement and attraction they initially felt for each other.

We were sitting on the lawn at an outdoor concert recently, listening to Diana Krall sing jazz.

The stars were coming out, the evening was balmy and calm—an equilibrium night. The music was magical, and the whole effect was magnificently romantic. We were on our weekly date, and we were in love—more than ever.

Decades ago, a relationship expert advised us to continue our courtship and go out on a date once each week. Then he promised us that if we would do that one simple thing—go out on a real date together once a week—that our love and commitment to each other would continue to grow.

Quite a challenge; quite a commitment; quite a promise.

When you courted your spouse, you thought about it, you planned it, and you strategized how to win her (or him). There was nothing you wouldn't do, no small touch or detail you wouldn't add, and no effort you wouldn't make. You sought to create romance!

Is it any less important now?

In your courtship, you worked hard and thought hard to find out what your partner liked most and what made the other happy. Is it any less important to know those things now—and to practice and implement them?

COMPATIBILITY

This word, often used today as a justification for cohabitation ("to see if we are physically and sexually compatible"), should instead be used in an emotional context. When a couple thinks of courtship and dating as a way of getting to know each other emotionally and mentally, compatibility becomes a wonderfully interesting and nuanced question. And when the emotional and mental compatibility is pursued first, the physical, sexual compatibility that comes later will be far more beautiful and rewarding. Then, as years go by, that closeness and compatibility have the inexhaustible potential to continue to deepen and expand.

Compatibility is not something you are tested on or something you "either have or you don't"; it is something you work on, something you develop, and something you gain—and keep on gaining—through deliberate and purposeful effort.

COMMITMENT

It is the chastity, courtship, and emotional compatibility that make total and joyous commitment possible. In a world that often associates commitment with a loss of freedom or independence, we need to know that exactly the opposite is true. When full, unqualified, and unconditional commitment is made to each other, it brings with it a wondrous liberation and peace that can't be found elsewhere. Everlasting but also forever capable of being renewed, exclusive commitment is the ultimate gift.

This one is so important, so pivotal, and so indispensable to happiness that all of Myth #6 is dedicated to this truth; the importance of attaining the full power of complete commitment.

CELEBRATION

We who have found the joy of committed marriage—not an endless conflict-free bliss but a worked-for, stay-at-it kind of happiness—need to celebrate it more! We need to be advocates for the five C's and let others know by our example and our attitudes that we have found the best, most efficient, most secure and joyous way to live.

Many people, when they read these brief overviews of the five C's, have two conflicting and opposite sensations. One is the tendency to reject them—to feel that some of them are outdated and not possible in today's world. The belief is that these five C's are so far from today's norms that they are not even worth considering.

But the other sensation is a longing—a certain attraction to the kind of honor, romance, and excitement that these five C's arouse in the back of our minds.

> *We are believers. We are converts to the wonder and beauty of this type of lifestyle. And we are practicing the fifth C right now, right here in this chapter—celebrating and expressing gratitude for what we believe is the happiest way to live. We suggest that it is available to everyone—at any life stage and with any history—if they are willing to work for it.*

5. The No-Waves Myth

(AND OTHER MYTHS AND TRUTHS ABOUT MARITAL COMMUNICATION.)

MYTH: In marriage some things are better left unsaid; and it's safest to float along and not make waves.

TRUTH: Unexpressed feelings never die; they just get buried and come forth later in uglier forms. Timing is important, but the best marriages communicate everything—even when it creates some turbulence.

1. SUB-MYTH: Too much of the wrong kind of communication can ruin a relationship, so share less.

   TRUTH: More often, it's too little of the right kind of communication that puts marriages in peril, so share more.

2. SUB-MYTH: Marriage kills excitement and romance; and relationships get stale and less passionate over time.

   TRUTH: Communication can rise to new levels after the marriage commitment, and steadily improve over time—lifting passion, romance, magic, and excitement with it.

3. SUB-MYTH: The hardest things to agree on are money, sex, goals, parenting methods, and religious beliefs.

   TRUTH: These five most common causes of divorce can be flipped into the five key subjects of good marriage communication.

4. SUB-MYTH: Marriage is serious business.

   TRUTH: Part of it sure is, but there had better be another part, because, from our experience, a sense of humor ranks number one in what is looked for in a spouse.

5-1: "DON'T MAKE WAVES"

We were lucky to have an incredible couple as our mentors for nearly fifty years. Stephen Covey and his wonderful wife, Sandra, were our teachers and later our neighbors. They were exactly fifteen years older than we were and had done so many of the same things we had—but fifteen years sooner. We would watch their marriage and family and project ourselves to that level in fifteen years.

One night over dinner, they dispensed with a myth and implanted a truth at the same time. Stephen posed a question to the two of us that was designed to make us think and to dissuade us from having a "no waves" goal for our marriage. He said, "I'm going to give you a choice between two catchy sayings about marriage, and you tell me which one you believe. You can only choose one, because they are mutually exclusive and you can't believe them both."

The first was: "Some things are better left unsaid."

And the second was: "Unexpressed feelings never die, they just get buried and come forth later in uglier forms."

Each of us were inclined to vote for both. Clearly you can't say everything you feel or think at every moment without initiating or escalating arguments and disrupting the love between you, but you certainly don't want to harbor things and not express feelings to the point that they begin to fester and gnaw at you.

But Covey insisted that we had to choose, because we couldn't do both. It was a long discussion, but in the end we came to understand that he thought the first quote was only true or valid in marriage as a matter of timing. "Some things are better left unsaid" in a heated moment, but they need expression before they "get buried and come forth later in uglier forms."

What he taught us that night was that a marriage is unlike any other relationship and has to be governed by different rules and principles than other relationships.

There are a lot of small bits of misplaced "marital wisdom" out there that didn't quite make our list of eight myths, but that are equally untrue and undesirably deceptive—especially concerning communication:

- "Agree to disagree."
- "There are enough tempests and storms in marriage, so don't make waves."
- "Just get past the tensions—ignore them until they go away."

Try to imagine a lake so calm and placid that there are never any wind or waves. It makes for a pretty unattractive and boring dream, and before long the lake starts to get stagnant and to smell. What if wind and waves are the real stuff of communication and lakes are cleaner and clearer after they are churned up a bit now and then by storms?

What if we should never worry about too much communication, only too little?

What if better communication, sharing, and unity result less from bottling things up and more from letting things out?

We actually think all of these are not what-ifs, but facts.

5-2: QUALITY AND QUANTITY OF COMMUNICATION

Linda: *I started out as a terrible communicator when dealing with my frustrations. When Richard and I were first married, my only example of communication in marriage was what I observed from my parents. My dad was thirteen years older than my mom and was a quiet, kind, hardworking farmer and a gentle soul. My mom on the other hand was a fabulous, driven, type A, elementary school teacher, athlete, and musician. We all knew when she was mad because she would slam the knife and fork drawer, sending the utensils flying inside and making a huge crash that made everyone cringe. We kids knew something was wrong but never just what it was—and we never saw any resolution. When my mom's sister visited every week or so, the two of them would retire to the bedroom while dad was at work and go over the frustrating things that both of their husbands had done since their last meeting. I'm not sure their husbands ever knew what they had done to offend their wives.*

I swore that I would never do that in my future marriage, but tradition flows deep; I had hardly unloaded our eating utensils in our first little student apartment before I found an opportunity to slam the knife and fork drawer!

When Richard would ask me what was wrong, I always replied, "Nothing!" Sometimes it took several days for me to be able to express my frustration. Sadly, those bad feelings were festering! I had no sister in Boston to share my frustrations with and with every new "incident" I became more and more angry. Finally, after a big explosion, Richard began the long journey of helping me to open my mouth and tell him what was bothering me. I've become so good over time that he may now wish he had not been such a good teacher!

Some couples blame their marriage problems on "too much":

- "We just love too much!"
- "We just say too much!"
- "We would be better off to just talk less, let some things go, and only communicate when it is good or positive communication."

There isn't such a thing as too much love, too much communication, or too much time in a marriage.

But it doesn't work that way. We can't limit the quantity of our communication and expect the quality of our communication to improve. The quality and quantity ultimately go together.

This marriaging myth is a little like a common parenting myth where parent says, "Well, I don't have much time to spend with my kid, but I try to make it quality time." Quality time is usually an excuse. The fact is that the quality of time spent together is often a product of the quantity of time spent together.

There isn't such a thing as too much love, too much communication, or too much time in a marriage. We should want all we can get of each of them and strive to increase them all. The quest, of course, is to find more of the right time, more of the best communication, and more of the strongest love.

5-3: CHANGING HOW YOU ACT AND REACT

Our minds are programmable. We can decide how we want to act and react and literally program those qualities into our brains.

One reason it is so difficult to come up with an actual plan to improve and strengthen our relationships is that communication involves a lot of responding and reacting. Most plans are about acting and initiating, not about responding and reacting.

If you are setting out to accomplish something, you can set up a straightforward plan to get it done, and then just go out and do it. With a relationship, though, it's not just about what you want or do. There is another person involved—another person who is different from you—who has different needs, expectations, and wants.

And as mentioned, it is so easy to start dwelling on what we would like to change about the other person. It's so easy for us to see what they could do better, how they could meet our needs, or how they could change little things that bug us.

With parenting, we find ourselves saying (or thinking) things like, "I want to be a better parent, so I've got to start changing my kids." In marriaging we think, "We could have a better marriage if only my spouse would change a couple of things."

Relationships are about how we act to *and* how we react toward another person.

We may even go to the other extreme and say things like, "I don't care what she does, I am just going to worry about me and do what I have to do whether she likes it or not."

Don't forget that a relationship is not just about you or just about the other person but about both of you, how you interrelate with each other, and how you have interdependencies, overlaps, and synergies.

Relationships are about how we act to *and* how we react toward another person.

Over the years, in thinking about how to deal proactively with a reactive process, we found some help from an unexpected source—Benjamin Franklin.

Good old Ben decided that he could choose a list of desirable qualities he wanted to incorporate into his personality and character—and then actually acquired them by concentrating on one quality at a time. He defined each quality clearly in his mind and then focused on it until it became a natural and integral part of who he was. Essentially, he programmed himself to be the possessor of the qualities he desired.

It is possible to do something similar with our own individual responses to those with whom we have important relationships. By deciding in advance on the kinds of reactions we will respond with and the characteristics we will exhibit in certain relationships, we can actually program them into our natures to the point that we will begin to manifest them subconsciously.

Let us give you an example: We know a father who came up with four words that described how he wanted to relate to his children—four words that expressed to his own mind what he wanted to project to his kids whenever he was around them. His words, with simple definitions were:

- *Calm:* I want to project peacefulness and patience and avoid anger and harshness.
- *Confidence:* I always believe in my kids and compliment them positively at every opportunity.
- *Consultant:* I help them make their own decisions and respect their agency rather than forcing them to obey.
- *Concentrate:* I focus on the child I am with and treat each one as a unique individual rather than comparing them to each other.

This dad, who was a runner, had the habit of reviewing his four words each morning as he jogged. He would say to himself "I am *calm* with my children" and then think of how he had been calm with them during the previous day. He did the same with each of his words each day, programming their qualities into his conscious and subconscious mind until he found himself modeling them and following them without thinking about it.

Richard: I tried to follow the same concept (and the same alliteration) in coming up with four words that I wanted to typify my relationship with Linda, and they were:

Partnership: *We want equality and more—we want oneness.*

Priority: *No one and no thing matters more than her, and I will incorporate that priority into everything I do and into how I approach my choices in everyday life. She comes first.*

Pamper and 'Preciate: *(I had to push the alliteration a bit on that one.) I love to care for her, to compliment her, and to express specific gratitude for the countless things she does for me.*

Protect: *Not to be in any way chauvinistic, but I do feel protective of Linda—and she protects me in many ways too. I want her to feel that I am always there for her.*

Come up with your own words—a short set of them for your relationship with your spouse, and another set for your relationship with your kids. Repeat, rehearse, and reinforce them in your mind each day during some repetitive activity like running, exercising, shaving, or showering. Gradually, you will find yourself taking on the qualities you have designed for yourself—qualities that will enhance and strengthen your most important relationships.

5-4: TURNING THE FIVE MOST COMMON REASONS FOR DIVORCE INTO YOUR FIVE STRONGEST TOPICS OF CONVERSATION

Most of us have seen studies or articles on the five prime causes of divorce:

- Money concerns
- Sexual issues
- Parenting differences
- Career or goal disagreements
- Moral or religious conflicts

An interesting juxtaposition is to view those five prime causes of divorce as the five things couples should be most conscientious about in terms of open and total communication—we can adopt them as the very five things that have to be communicated about almost constantly in a strong marriage.

Think about that juxtaposition for a moment: The five things that are most commonly blamed for divorce are the very five things that have to be the topics of open, ongoing communication if a marriage is to be strong. Consistent, candid conversation about each of the

The five things that are most commonly blamed for divorce are the very five things that need the most marital communication.

five is what will turn the topics into strengths and elements of unity instead of problems that can lead to separation or divorce.

Some will say, "Can't we each have our own finances—why share everything?" Or, "Why do we have to talk about sex—can't we just do it?" Or, "She's strict with the kids and I'm not—we just agree to disagree."

But most of us understand that these five things, if they go unresolved and undiscussed, can bring down a marriage. Yet if they are openly, deliberately, and almost constantly talked about, they can bring the understanding and empathy—if not the agreement—that can keep a marriage strong.

So, when? How? Where do we talk consistently and continuously about these five things? A few ideas:

- Try to go to bed together at the same time to facilitate "pillow talk."
- Go on a weekly date and continue your courtship as well as your communication about these five issues.
- Have a weekly Sunday Session, or meeting between just the two of you, once a week where you discuss the schedule and goals for the next week. Once a month, make your session more of a little getaway to plan the month. Then, take a short trip together once a year to set goals for the year ahead. Incorporate into all of these an ongoing conversation about the five key discussion topics. Make the list of topics part of your agenda. (More on this later.)
- Pray together every night, or meditate if you don't pray, and include the five topics.

- Remember the truth in this section and make it your motto: "Unexpressed feelings never die; they just get buried and come forth later in uglier forms."

The fact that we know what the five most common reasons are for divorce does not mean that we should fear them, it means we should be warned by them and proactively make them the five things we work hardest to communicate about.

5-5: LISTENING TO
EACH OTHER

It turns out that it is your ears that can improve your relation-ship, not your tongue.

An underlying problem with most relationships is that one key word we know so well but sometimes practice so little—listening!

Let us toss out ten listening ideas that we think have merit. Pick from the list the ones you feel you could improve on or that seem like they would work for you:

1. Make eye contact. Let your spouse see that you are really paying attention.

2. Ask the right kind of questions, which often use the words "how" and "feel." ("*How* did that make you *feel*?") Ask questions that make your spouse think and that can't be answered with one word.

3. Learn to use the word "Really?" It can be said in dozens of different intonations and usually extends and deepens a conversation. It can imply surprise, praise, agreement, or empathy, and it just shows that you are listening and encourages the other to keep on talking.

4. Even better than the word "really" is the technique of sim-ply re-phrasing what your spouse has just said. Don't judge

or solve or end anything, just repeat it back in your own words so that your spouse knows that you were listening and feels encouraged to go on.

5. Take advantage of the time you are in the car together. Turn the radio off and ask good questions. Your spouse can't get up and walk away and neither can you.

6. As mentioned, use "pillow time" as listening time—when you are relaxed and tired and both have your guard down.

7. Praise and reward each other's questions. Quick or dismissive answers to a spouse's questions are opportunities wasted. Start by saying, "Great question," and then add something like, "What do you think the answer is?" Turn it into as long of a discussion as you have time for, and then suggest that you continue the talk later or perhaps do some research on it together.

8. Include each other in any social media you use. Also, have joint social media accounts when possible—pages that you share and that you both post on. Follow each other and follow the same others.

9. Try to say "no" less. We have a good friend who offered to give his wife a dollar every time he said the word "no" just to get him out of the habit. It cost him a little money, but he soon got over it and found that there were other, nicer ways to reply in the negative when he had to. Too often we say "no" (or "no, no, n-n-n-no") too quickly to express disagreement or disapproval—before we have taken the time to listen.

10. Ask each other to tell you their "happy" for the day and their "sad" for the day—and tell them yours.

Oh, the power that comes and the love that is shown by listening. We all know listening is the key to better communication and hopefully these ideas, or others that they will bring to your mind, will help you to do ot just a little bit better.

5-6: BEING FUNNY–LAUGHTER IS AN INSTANT VACATION

Linda: I remember as a young girl thinking that the one thing I wanted most in my future husband was a sense of humor. "If he can make me laugh," I thought, "everything else will work out."

Polls show that I wasn't alone in that wish. Having a sense of humor is often the number one criteria of what makes a good marriage partner.

It is certainly a key to good marital communication.

One of our favorite ideas for finding an appropriate marriage partner is from Will Ferrell. "Before you marry a person, you should first make them use a computer with slow internet to see who they really are."[1]

The wise Henry Ward Beecher said, "A person without a sense of humor is like a wagon without springs. It's jolted by every pebble on the road."[2]

It's so true that being able to get through the crazy daily events of our lives with a little humor relieves the jolts and makes life so much easier. The gift of making something funny instead of letting it become a point of irritation is priceless.

Linda: My dad was a master of wit and made himself endearing by using his great sense of humor. When he was annoyed because I had walked into the room where he was watching TV and stopped inadvertently directly in front of his view, instead of being openly annoyed, he would quietly say, "Well Linda, you make a better door than a window." This always brought a giggle.

When Bob Hope was ninety-five, he was asked about the secret of his longevity. He said, "Everyone tells you it's diet and exercise. But laughter is it. Laughter is therapy . . . an instant vacation!"[3]

Zach Brittle in *The Gottman Relationship Blog* says, "If laughter is what makes us human, then humor is a necessary tie that binds us to one another and reminds us that our relationships are designed to bring joy. Monty Python's John Cleese, who understands humor more than most, says, 'A wonderful thing about true laughter is that it just destroys any kind of system of dividing people.'"[4]

Others agree: "Laugh out loud," says Chuck Swindoll. "It helps flush out the nervous system." On another occasion Chuck said, "Laughter is the most beautiful and beneficial therapy God ever granted humanity."

Arnold Glasow said, "Laughter is a tranquilizer with no side effects."[5]

As married couples—particularly if we have kids—our lives are filled with things that are either riotously funny or stunningly frustrating, depending on how we look at them. These things come in large and small sizes. Next time all three kids spill their milk at the same meal, remember the truth that "crisis plus time equals humor." It

> **Our lives are filled with things that are either riotously funny or stunningly frustrating, depending on how we look at them.**

will be funny when you look back on it later. Finding the humor and appreciating it—and making each other laugh—is one of the most important skills we can gain.

With three adult children and their families living close to us right now, a lot of crazy random things happen that can't be anticipated or planned for. Often, these situations start out to be simple but somehow become so complex that it is ridiculous—that's just how family life is. In those moments, we have to either laugh or cry; if the situation is not life-threatening, we usually choose to laugh.

At Thanksgiving last year, our wonderful daughter-in-law Kristi—who had been without her husband for two weeks because of his international business trip—offered to bring thirty pounds of potatoes and a pretzel Jell-O salad (sounds strange but it is delicious) to our enormous forty-person feast. She and her just-returned husband piled their six kids in their big Sprinter and were about halfway along on the one-hour drive to our house when they realized that they forgot the potatoes. They whipped the car around and went back for them and texted us on their way back so we wouldn't worry. Kristi said that the kids were peeling the potatoes in the back of the Sprinter and that their six-year-old Bennett had just stepped in the Jell-O salad. However, her phone autocorrected so that her text said, "The kids are in the back peeing the potatoes." That great mom was all smiles when the kids brought in the peeled potatoes and beautifully smushed pretzel Jell-O salad. What a great laugh we had!

Linda: *Richard and I also love all the inside jokes that we have accumulated through our many years together. Just one word between us on certain things is enough to make us both laugh. We always know exactly what the other is thinking.*

For example, when we eat out together, Richard always wants a different table than the first one offered, and he is always hungry when we arrive and likes to say, "We're ready to order"—even though we haven't looked at the menu yet. When we do, he usually can't decide between two things and suggests that I order one of them.

On that food subject, we now smile and roll our eyes whenever we take our foodie daughters to dinner. Literally twenty minutes after we have been seated with menus in our hands, these girls will have gone through every possible option on the menu and are still pondering what they might miss when they choose just one thing. When Richard and I start laughing, they know what it means. Maybe this indecision is the result of all those years of drive-through windows at fast food places with all our little kids when their dad would ignore all of their requests and just order a slew of hamburgers, some fries, and a dozen waters for the crew in the back. For many years, it was way too hard to offer options to our whole motley crew. There was always some griping, but it saved time, confusion, and lots of fighting! Even thinking about it now makes us laugh. I love these inside jokes.

5-7: AN EXECUTIVE SESSION FOR TOP MANAGEMENT

Early in our marriage, at the suggestion of a wise mentor, we started having a Sunday Session each week as a couple. We would go through the schedule for the week ahead, do a little evaluating of the week just passed, try to clear up any unresolved issues in our relationship, and deal with any concerns we had about the kids.

Sometimes the simplest key to better communication is just to have a meeting!

The top management in a two-parent family would be those two parents. Perhaps the wife could be the CEO and the dad could be the CFO, or vice versa.

Like any top management team, they would probably want to have an Executive Session once a week to review how things are going, set some goals, and perhaps make a few policy adjustments.

Holding these regular meetings might improve your family's organization and generate better results. It might cut down scheduling conflicts and get both managers on the same page. And it might even improve the relationship between the two managers as they work together on their common interests and objectives.

In our case, at first, it seemed a little odd to have a meeting with the person you live with, but the longer we did it, the more we realized how much we needed it—and the more hooked we got on holding it "religiously" each Sunday. In fact, we decided that living together was the very reason we did have to schedule an actual meeting; it was a time we could count on to get a little more organized and to communicate a little better.

At that point in our lives, we decided that Linda was the general partner for what went on inside the home, or the "inner partner," and Richard was the "outer partner," dealing with what went on outside the home. We had equal ownership in both but would each give a little report or update on our domain, since we spent more of our time and energy there.

We also added an element to our Sunday Sessions that we simply called "testimonies." During this time, we would each take a few moments to express our feelings and beliefs to the other. This quickly became our favorite aspect of the weekly sessions, because it was when positive feelings were expressed and negative feelings were aired out and resolved. And we found that in the somewhat structured and spiritual setting of our weekly meeting, offense was seldom taken and any festering feelings were let out and cleared up.

We figured out that even the setting and environment for our Sunday Session mattered. If a high-level management meeting were held at the water cooler or in the hall, it wouldn't be as effective or meaningful as if you held it in the boardroom or the executive office. Likewise, we found that if we just chatted in the car on the way to church or made a couple of catch-up comments on the way to bed, the experience was nowhere near as effective as actually sitting down in a conducive setting at a specific time.

In those first years, we would meet at the kitchen table or at the desk in our den, and the meeting was usually early, before the kids woke up, or late, after they had gone to bed. More recently, we sit down at our "Taj Table"—an inlaid black marble table we shipped back from a stonemason's shop in Agra, India, near the Taj Mahal. The table lends a certain gravity and weight to our meetings, or at least we imagine that it does. We recommend finding a special place for you and conducting your Executive Sessions there.

It's something that all of us know—that our marriages are our most important relationships and that our families are our highest priorities—and having a regular weekly meeting about how to focus and improve in our marriages and families can provide the reminders and refreshers that can help us to do a little better on them both.

Here is an outline of topics that may help you structure your own weekly Sunday Session:

1. Coordinate your schedules and priorities for the upcoming week so that you are together when you need to be and know where each other is when you are apart.

2. Decide on one night during the coming week when you will go on a date, which might be as complete as dinner and a movie or as simple as a little walk or drive together. Think of it as a continuation of your courtship; be willing to make the time sacrifice and pay the price for a babysitter.

3. Spend a moment on each of the five critical areas of marital communication (from Chapter 5-4) and see if there are any aspects that need more discussion or resolution.

4. Have a private testimony meeting or feelings session where each of you takes a few minutes to tell the other your feelings about your goals, your relationship concerns, your faith, and your love. Listen attentively to the other person

when it is his or her turn and express yourself honestly when it is yours.

5. Finish with a prayer, meditation, or whatever spiritual conclusion feels comfortable to you. If you do pray out loud together, have each of you be the voice for a part of the prayer. Whether or not this prayer is a regular or usual process in your marriage, do it to close your weekly Sunday Session.

There are 168 hours in a week, and you can spare one of them for the most important relationship of your life.

Giving this gift to each other—a weekly Sunday Session or Executive Session—will take real commitment, and it will take an hour that you may not think you have. But there are 168 hours in a week, and you can spare one of them for the most important relationship of your life.

5-8: THE FIVE-FACET REVIEW

People occasionally ask us, "If you could recommend just one thing to parents or to marriage partners, what would it be?"

We love something called the five-facet review *because it has such positive impacts on both parenting and on marriaging.*

Set aside one evening each month to go to dinner someplace—just a nice dinner date—and talk exclusively about your children. If you have a blended family, this will be an invaluable exercise as you listen to what the genetic parent knows and what the "new parent" perceives about each child.

But in any case, simply go out together—just the two of you, away from the very children you are going to talk about—and preferably to a place where you won't get distracted or meet too many people you know. Then have an organized, comprehensive discussion about your children where you go through the five facets with each of your kids: physical, mental, social, emotional, and spiritual. Have a five-facet notebook that you take each month that carries the conversation over from one month to the next and allows you to follow up on whatever plans or notes you made the month before.

Here is a brief example of how such a conversation could go: "How is Brandon doing physically?" Talk through any issues, from weight to teeth to eyes. How about exercise, sports, and activity level—any health problems? If there is an issue, focus in on it and brainstorm about it. If it's all good, move on. "How is he doing mentally?" Talk about school, about how he learns, and where his mental gifts are. Take notes about concerns and about what you intend to do about any concerns (and about who will do it). "How is he doing socially?" Discuss friends and how he interacts, isolating any areas that need attention. "How is he doing emotionally?" What are danger signs? How does he handle things? Is he ever too moody? What upsets him? And finally ask, "How is he doing spiritually?" Discuss how his heart and his faith are doing—where is he doing well and where does he need help?

Take notes and think together. When you discover and isolate a concern, decide who will do what about it, knowing you will revisit it in your next month's five-facet review. It is amazing that once you focus on something as a couple, ideas and solutions will come to you readily. Give each other assignments (e.g., Mom to Dad: "Can you read with David twice a week this month? You'll see that he isn't on grade level with his reading skills.").

You know more about your kids than you think you do, and your spouse knows more than you think he or she does about each child. It just takes a discussion and some brainstorming and questions to pull out things you didn't even know you knew.

As a marriaging, parenting couple, you will come up with specific things to work on each month, and they will be *your* thoughts—you, as the real and only experts on your child. The things you think of and the inspiration you receive will be much more useful (and much more specifically geared to your child) than anything you will ever find in a parenting book. The real work of parenting is putting together the puzzle that each child represents. Each child

The real work of parenting is putting together the puzzle that each child represents.

is a unique individual that comes as who they are, but your aware-
ness, monitoring, and guidance all along the way can be facilitated
by this kind of five-facet analysis.

Additionally, the conclusions and discovered needs of your
five-facet review may be special material for your prayers, ongoing
meditation, and thoughts about each of your children.

A regular five-facet review can be a tremendous help in parenting. However, the reason we are talking about it here is that it
can also be a wonderful strengthening influence on a marriage. We
often suggest this five-facet review as a great way to get one parent
more involved in the parenting process. A less-involved parent can
become a great problem-solver once a problem is recognized and a
great coach once the specific potential of a child is seen or discussed.

When two people are working, thinking, and talking together
about something of great value to both of them, it cannot help but
draw them closer. As your parenting partnership thrives, so will
your marriaging.

*Now that we are empty nesters, we have continued this tra-
dition. When we are on a plane or in the car for a long drive,
we enjoy doing five-facet reviews of our grown children. It's a
different dynamic, but it can be so fun to consider the small
needs or things we might find to help our children. They're still
our kids!*

*Occasionally, we also find it insightful to consider our own
personal five facets during an Executive Session. It's fun to
talk with each other about how we think we are each doing
physically, socially, emotionally, mentally, and spiritually.*

6. The Test-Drive Myth

(AND OTHER MYTHS AND TRUTHS ABOUT MARITAL COMMITMENT.)

MYTH: You wouldn't buy a car until you had taken a test drive, and it is unwise to make a marriage commitment before you have lived together long enough to know if it will work.

TRUTH: It is the commitment that will make a marriage work. Real security comes from promising and implementing complete allegiance, not from conditional, tentative try-it-and-see.

1. **SUB-MYTH: Formal commitments don't matter. We don't need some license or certificate or ink on paper to be in love and live together.**

   TRUTH: Formally married couples have twice as high a chance of being together in ten years as those without the "ink on paper."

2. **SUB-MYTH: The longer you wait and the older you are when you get married, the better your marriage will be.**

   TRUTH: There is no one-size-fits-all or one ideal age for marriage. It's more about preparation and commitment than it is about how old you are.

3. **SUB-MYTH: The more relationships I have, the more likely I will be to find the right one—the one that will last.**

   TRUTH: Several uncommitted relationships will never add up to one committed one.

6-1: ARE YOU "IN A RELATIONSHIP" OR "IN A COMMITMENT"?

We recently had a conversation with an associate who is living with his girlfriend. We asked him if they were planning to get married.

"Well, we hope to, if everything works out," he said. "We just want to live together long enough to be sure we are compatible before we make a commitment."

In the conversation, he used a cliché that we don't like: "You wouldn't want to buy a car before you had taken it on a test drive."

We didn't know him well enough to start giving advice, but we would have loved to tell him (and if we get better acquainted, maybe we will) that he and his girlfriend's chances of it "working out" are less than half of what they would be if they were married. We would also have liked to tell him that even if and when they do get married, their chances of divorce will be higher than if they had not cohabitated before marriage.

But the biggest thing we wanted to tell him has to do with commitment—when it should come and what it can do for a relationship and for a marriage. His view of commitment—as something you do after you are sure that the relationship will work out—is backward.

In truth, commitment is the one thing that can cause the relationship to work out.

For many years, we have taught a seminar on prioritizing relationships above everything else in life. The word "relationship" has become, to us, one of the most important words in the English language. And of course—in our minds at least—the marriage relationship is the most important of all.

But over the last decade or two, the word has taken on a new meaning that we don't like—a meaning that, in some ways, connotes the very opposite of what we think the word should mean. We remember one of the first times a certain juxtaposition got our attention. In the Question and Answer phase of our seminar, a young man raised his hand and started his question with "I'm currently in a relationship . . . ." The connotation was that relationships are things you can move into and out of, like apartments. In one today, in another one tomorrow, moving out whenever you don't like it anymore.

In today's vernacular, "a relationship" has become the alternative to "a commitment."

Strangely then, "a relationship" has become the alternative to "a commitment."

A relationship in this new vernacular is temporary, without a set term or span of time; something conditional and transitory and unpredictable. A relationship is a trial balloon, something that we will blow up to see if it holds air, something that could pop at any moment.

Where is the power in such a relationship? Where is the security? Where is the learning and the growing? And where is the joy that only comes from enduring the ups and downs and from finding a way to make things work.

Where is the "in sickness and health" and the "in good times and bad"? Where is the durability and the resilience that, over time, grow into a love deeper and more exciting than any erotic fling?

Are you in a relationship? Or are you in a commitment?

Commitment is not a culmination. It is a strong beginning.

Commitment is not something you do after you have made it through the hard times. It is the thing that will get you through the hard times.

Commitment is not a nice celebration you have if or when you decide you can be happy together. It is the thing that makes it possible to be happy together.

Commitment is not something you do after you have made it through the hard times. It is the thing that will get you through the hard times.

The reason people are afraid of commitments is that they involve risk and vulnerability. When you commit to someone in a way as visible and public as marriage, you risk that it won't work and that it will be hard to get out of the relationship; you give up some of your "freedom"; you eliminate some options. You get into a situation that requires some sacrifice and some extra responsibility.

The easy way is to just live together, just try it out, leave yourself a back door. Nothing ventured, nothing gained. Easy come, easy go.

But when nothing is risked, nothing is gained. High risk, high reward; low risk, low reward.

You have heard that marriage is not for the fainthearted. We agree with that. Marriage is for the adventurous. Marriage is for the risk-takers.

But the irony is that our odds get better as we take that risk.

6-2: THE MAGIC OF TOTAL COMMITMENT

We are writing this chapter from the middle of the Mediterranean, where we are speaking on a cruise ship. And as luck would have it, the magic show in the ship's theater gave us the metaphor we were looking for.

Real, nothing-held-back marriage commitments actually become a kind of magic. It is the magic of synergy—of a combination where the total is greater than the sum of its parts; where one plus one can equal more than two. Much more.

A year earlier in Philadelphia, we were reminded of this kind of magic by singer and songwriter John Legend, who was the commencement speaker at our son's graduation from UPenn. He talked about his song "All of Me." It's a song about the magic of commitment where "all of me loves all of you."

Of course, marriage can be thought of as a responsibility, which it certainly is. It can be thought of as a duty and as a sacrifice and as a challenge, too, all of which would be accurate. And these same words would also be fitting descriptions for the children and family that usually come with marriage.

But if those were the only contexts for marriage, we might miss the most important and the most fantastic aspects of what marriage is and what it can be. We might miss the "all of me loves all of you" part. And we might miss the magic of knowing marriage as synergy, adventure, and the ultimate security and joy.

We know of a very successful coach who seemed to be able to create a winning team out of mediocre talent—every season. When asked how he did it, he said, "It's all about the commitment." Commitment, in his mind, meant loyalty, teamwork, and unwavering determination. Total commitment, he said, was much more rare than talent. Commitment meant you never gave up, no matter what the score and no matter how long the odds. Commitment meant you cared more about the team than about yourself.

To that coach, courage, risk, devotion, and determination were all manifest in the concept of commitment. It was what got you through tough situations. It was what freed you from doubt and from second-guessing. It was what made you "all in" and banished any thought that perhaps this was not the right game or the right team for you.

It can be the same in marriage. Once there is total commitment, things become much more simple and positive. When disagreements happen, you do what you have to do to work through them—there is no thought of jumping ship or second-guessing about whether you knew each other well enough before marriage. Total commitment is unquestioned, and it is so strong that it makes molehills out of what could otherwise be mountains.

When marriage is built on total commitment—when we absolutely mean our vows of "in sickness and in health" and "for better or worse"—life takes on a certain purpose and clarity. Bailing out or giving up is never an

Once there is total commitment, things become much more simple and positive.

option, so you don't waste time or mental energy contemplating it. You just work through things, believing in each other and believing in your commitment.

Don't fall into the trap of saying you don't need "some ceremony" or "some ink stains on a piece of paper" to prove your commitment. Don't look for ways to commit without formalities and rings and vows. Instead, look for *more* of these symbols to safeguard and solidify your commitment. Marriage is the ultimate manifestation of commitment.

Not all marriages will last, or should last, and perhaps some should never have happened. However, the best chance marriages have come via total commitment. It makes you strong. It makes you resilient. It frees up your mind and your heart to know things and feel things you couldn't access without it.

And it allows you to give your partner the greatest gift and the most profound security imaginable—the gift of yourself and the security of knowing that you will always be hers—only hers—and she will always be yours—only yours.

That is magic.

6-3: NEVER UNDERVALUE COMMITMENT OR RECOMMITMENT

We were speaking to a group on the island of Maui and staying in a lovely hotel where the event was held. We were interested that on the grounds of the hotel there was a beautiful little wedding chapel that seemed to be busy all day long. In looking into it, we found that while there were many marriages performed there, the biggest business it did was recommitment ceremonies. We talked to some of the couples that were there for a recommitment ceremony and several said it was something they did every few years—a retaking of their vows, a re-establishment of the sanctity of their union and the priority of their marriage, and an additional ceremony to remind them of their love for and total commitment to each other.

There is a troubling pattern that we sometimes see in marriages, and it can affect us all:

In our young adult years, we fall in love, begin our families, and experience the joys and sorrows that come with the risks of committed, caring relationships. But often, as we move toward midlife, we can grow impatient, disillusioned, or just tired, and allow some combination of selfishness, foolishness, and fatigue to turn us away from our spouse or child. Alternatively, we may simply stop

> **When real commitment is felt and expressed, it has a way of shrinking problems–of making them look manageable.**

putting forth the necessary effort and let our family relationships gradually slip and slide away. If either of these be the case, we may realize in later life that what we gave up was everything and what we traded it for is nothing.

It is often in this midlife (sometimes very early midlife, this time of potential slippage and selfishness) that we need a purposeful and powerful recommitment to relationships.

We tend to undervalue and underestimate commitment. We forget about its pervasive power. When real commitment is felt and expressed, it has a way of shrinking problems—of making them look manageable. When commitment is thought of as unalterable, lasting, and unconditional, problems can't stand up to it—they can't match it in strength and permanence. Whatever the forces are that undermine relationships and break up families, they tend to back off in the presence of deep, complete commitment as though they had a mind of their own—and choose to go work on someone else where there is less commitment and where they can do more damage.

When there is commitment, true commitment, it fortifies a marriage and a family in truly remarkable ways. When adversity strikes a family—be it in the form of illness, accident, economic hardship, or anything else—if commitment is strong, the adversity strengthens that family and brings its members closer together instead of tearing it apart.

On the other hand, families without strong commitment are broken by adversity.

Right in our own neighborhood, we have seen clear manifestations of both strength and weakness in adversity. One couple was hit hard with illness and adversity, suffering both a case of cancer and a case of Parkinson's. They pulled together in a remarkable way and became more united than ever before in this time of crisis. Another family basically fell apart when some addiction problems emerged; the couple split up and the teenaged kids shot off in rebellious paths. We know both families well enough to see clearly that the difference in their reactions was the level of marital commitment that existed. With the first family—where commitment was strong and unquestioned—the adversity pulled them together; with the other family—where commitment was conditional—the adversity pulled them apart.

Commitment turns our hearts, *locking* them on the relationships that matter. If we want to fix our families, to shore them up against the distractions and dangers of today's world, and to preserve them for our old age, we must start with recommitment. Let the recommitment start in our hearts, and then we'll be capable of sending it out through our words and eyes to reassure and bless the lives of those we love most.

The real question, of course, is how we *apply* commitment or recommitment. After we profess it to those we love most, how do we demonstrate it in everyday life? The answer, and actually the beauty of it, is that different people will apply it in different ways. If your recommitment is *real*, it will manifest itself in ways that are tailored to your own situation and your own spouse and family's unique needs. The techniques are not as important as the heart; the mechanisms are not as important as the commitment.

6-4: LOVE, MARRIAGE, SEX–STILL THE BEST SEQUENCE

None of this chapter is intended to project guilt or judgement on anyone or on their premarital sexual activity—it is just to remind us all, regardless of what stage of marriage or pre-marriage we are in, that a commitment or a profound recommitment to the one we love is the most powerful and relationship-protecting thing we can do.

As mentioned, the "prevailing wisdom" in the world today is that it is foolish and impulsive to just marry someone you have never lived with, hoping you will be compatible.

Why not cohabitate for a while and test each other out before tying the knot?

While there are still couples who wait for a deep level of commitment before living together or sleeping together, today it is far more common for two people to explore their sexual compatibility before making long-term plans together.

So, which approach or method leads to better marriages? Sex and cohabitation before marriage or delaying them both until after marriage?

A new study (titled "RELATE") in the American Psychological Association's *Journal of Family Psychology* sides with a delayed approach.

The study involved 2,035 married individuals who participated in a popular online marital assessment.

The extensive questionnaire included the question, "When did you become sexual in this relationship?"

A statistical analysis showed the following benefits were enjoyed by couples who waited until marriage compared to those who started having sex in the early part of their relationship:

- Relationship stability was rated 22 percent higher.
- Relationship satisfaction was rated 20 percent higher.
- Sexual quality of the relationship was rated 15 percent better.
- Communication was rated 12 percent better.
- For couples who fell somewhere in between—who became sexually involved later in the relationship but prior to marriage—the benefits were about half as strong, but at least 10 percent higher in each category than those who began their relationship together by having sex.[1]

In other words—statistically—the longer you wait, the longer your marriage will last and the better it will be. There are exceptions of course, but on average, waiting seems to have some measurable benefits.

Noted in the study, Dean Busby, a professor at Brigham Young University in the School of Family Life said, "There's more to a relationship than sex, but we did find that those who waited longer were happier with the sexual aspect of their relationship. . . . I think it's because they've learned to talk and have the skills to work with issues that come up."

Sociologist Mark Regnerus of the University of Texas at Austin, who was not involved with this research, read the study and shared his take on the findings:

Couples who hit the honeymoon too early—that is, prioritize sex promptly at the outset of a relationship—often

Chastity is not only about morality; it is about practicality too.

find their relationships under-developed when it comes to the qualities that make relationships stable and spouses reliable and trustworthy.[2]

So the simple fact is that what we see in today's movies, romantic comedies, and TV sitcoms—where everyone jumps into bed on their first date—is actually *wrong* on at least three levels.

1. In the eyes of many, it is morally wrong.
2. It is wrong on a practical level because, as statistics show, marriage works better when sex is delayed.
3. It is factually wrong in that it doesn't really happen that way as often as the media suggests.

As parents, we ought to be teaching all three of these "wrongs" to our children. And we ought to be learning them profoundly for ourselves. The wonderful principle of chastity is not only about morality; it is about practicality too.

Kids need to know that just because they see newly acquainted people sleeping together in movies or on sitcoms, it doesn't mean that that's the way it usually happens—and it certainly doesn't need to be the way it happens for you and your family.

Other studies show that married couples that cohabitate prior to marriage are twice as likely to divorce than those that do not. So even among the third that gets married within three years of cohabitating, chances are good that that marriage will not last.

The nationwide *divorce* rate has actually leveled off and even declined slightly in recent years; but cohabitation without marriage and chosen singleness are growing dramatically and are pushing *marriage* rates to their lowest levels in history.

Of course, some cases of cohabitation work out well and lead to marriage and stable families, but as the saying goes "the odds are against it."

Consider some of the findings in the study released in 2018 from the National Center for Health Statistics of the US Department of Health and Human Services. A US poll was conducted of over 12,000 women between fifteen and forty-four years of age:

Of the 12,000 women, 29 percent had not lived with a man. Of the remaining women who had, 23 percent moved in with the man when they married him and 48 percent simply cohabitated, living with a man to whom they were not married.

In other words, of all the first unions that occurred, more than two-thirds were cohabitations and less than one-third were marriages. Another way of saying it: More than twice as many couples initially moved in together unmarried as did after they were married.

In an earlier version of the same study, done less than twenty years ago, the figures were shockingly different with 26 percent who had not lived with a man, 34 percent who cohabitated for their first union, and 40 percent who married before living with someone.[3]

So, in less than two decades, the number of couples who cohabitate first has soared by nearly 40 percent while those who marry first has declined by more than 40 percent.

The poll finds that after two to three years roughly one-third of cohabitating couples have married, one-third have broken up, and one-third continues to live together unmarried. And an increasing percentage (now about 21 percent) of cohabitating couples have a child within their first two years of living together—a child who is born to parents with a one-in-three chance of breaking up while the child is still a baby.

Other studies show that married couples that cohabitate prior to marriage are more likely to divorce than those that do not—some say twice as likely.[4] So even among the third that get married after cohabitating, the chances are reduced that the marriage will last and that it will provide a stable home for a child.

Besides the immediate statistical peril to both children and couples, there are other fundamental problems with cohabitation:

- It both replaces and weakens marriage as suggested above.
- It treats a partner like a car or a vacuum cleaner that ought to be used or test-driven before it is committed to.
- It stems from "individual freedom and options" rather than from responsibility, commitment, and children's needs. Selfishness prevails over sacrifice.
- It doesn't unite or combine families like marriage does. You don't gain cousins, uncles, in-laws, and extended families through cohabitation.
- It doesn't bring about resilience and reconciliation. The tendency and the impulse when things turn sour is to cut and run rather than to hang in there and resolve.
- It feeds on itself. People who have cohabitated once are more likely to do it again, and each time the chance of maintaining a long-term committed relationship goes down.

Here are three conclusive points taken from a scholarly study conducted by a friend of ours Dr. Jason Carroll, a university professor who has spent much of his professional life researching relationships:

The longer a dating couple waits to have sex, the better their relationship is after marriage. In fact, couples who wait until marriage to have sex report higher relationship satisfaction (20 percent higher), better communication patterns (12 percent better), less consideration of divorce (22 percent lower), and better sexual quality (15 percent better) than those who started having sex early in their dating. . . .

Early sex creates a sort of counterfeit intimacy that makes two people think they are closer to each other than they really are. This can cause people to "fall in love" with, and possibly even marry, someone who is not a good choice for them in the long run. . . . You have a better chance of making good decisions in dating when you have not become sexually involved with your dating partner. . . .

Sexual restraint benefits couples because it requires partners to prioritize communication and commitment as the foundation of their attraction to each other. This gives a different type of foundation from couples who build their relationship on physical attraction and sexual gratification.[5]

We asked someone who we knew had cohabitated prior to his marriage if these statistics made him feel bad. "On the contrary," he said, "those statistics make me feel somewhat lucky that my marriage has worked out so well despite the odds, and they make me want to go straight home and recommit to my wife right now."

6-5: THE EXCITEMENT AND ADVENTURE OF ACTUAL DATING AND ACTUAL MARRIAGE

As we write this chapter, we have recently finished a short visit with our youngest son, Eli. He lives in Manhattan with his wife, Julie, and their three adorable little kids. And we will soon board a plane to visit our youngest daughter, Charity; her new husband, Ian Wright; and their two baby boys (naturally we call them the Wright Brothers), who all live in London.

If you were to ask Eli, who is a world traveler and an extreme sports kind of guy, to tell you about his most exciting experiences, what do you think he would say? Or if you asked Charity—who traveled around the world in eighty days on her honeymoon—to share her greatest adventure, what would she tell you?

Both say essentially the same thing: Everything else pales when compared to the excitement, unpredictability, and adventure of being married and having children.

One of the most frequent reasons we hear from the millennial generation for avoiding marriage, or at least delaying it for a long time, is that they still want excitement, independence, freedom, and adventure in their lives.

They also want some peace and solitude.

And they think they would throw all of that out the window if they "settled down" and got married and had a family.

Let's talk about that excitement and adventure part—and the part about peace.

While skydiving or kite surfing or traveling the globe might seem adventurous and exciting, they fade almost into insignificance when compared to the ultimate adventure of marriage and the incomparable excitement of bringing a child into the world.

We know that everyone has their own timing and that there is no one-size-fits-all formula for marriage and family. We are all unique, and our way (or Eli's way or Charity's way) is not necessarily the best way for you. But if you want adventure and excitement, deliberately making the commitment of marriage is like jumping off a cliff. The risk and the rush are breathtaking. And fighting through the inevitable differences and difficulties is the challenge of a lifetime, with potential rewards that outshine any gold medal.

> Family life, particularly with kids, is like surfing a wave. Sometimes you wipe out. And even when you do ride one all the way to the beach, there is constant adjusting, weight shifting, and rebalancing.

The irony is that many are avoiding marriage today because they think it will be dull. Ask one hundred married people if marriage is dull and see if you can find one who says it is. Ask Charity or Eli about it.

Hard? Yes. Often unpleasant? Yes. Containing doubts and a certain amount of second-guessing? Yes.

But dull? Never!

Family life, particularly with kids, is like surfing a wave. Sometimes you wipe out. And even when you do ride one all the way

> There is no peace, no calm satisfaction, and no welling joy like simply holding hands with someone you love more than yourself, someone you have committed yourself to forever.

to the beach, there is constant adjusting, weight shifting, and rebalancing. You are always in danger of hitting something or losing the curl. But when you catch a perfect wave, and the pipeline opens up and it's just you and the energy of the ocean, it makes it all worth it.

And you are up at dawn the next morning to have the adventure again.

Teddy Roosevelt hoped to never be among "those cold and timid souls who neither know victory nor defeat." Instead, he wanted to be one "who is actually in the arena, whose face is marred by dust and sweat and blood; who strives valiantly; who errs, who comes short again and again, because there is no effort without error and short-coming; but who does actually strive to do the deeds; who knows the great enthusiasms, the great devotions; who spends himself in a worthy cause."

Did you ever hear a better description of what it is like to have and live with a marriage and a family every day? Is there any better name than "arena" for the turmoil and unpredictability and won-derful little moments of triumph in a young family?

Additionally, there is no peace, no calm satisfaction, and no well-ing joy like simply holding hands with someone you love more than yourself, someone you have committed yourself to forever. And there is no happiness like seeing your own child succeed at some-thing—or just watching him or her sleep at the end of a hard day.

We live in a time when two of the greatest delights and joys of all time are being abandoned: dating and marriage. Too many kids "hang out" or "hook up" or move around in groups but don't actually date. You know that thing called "dating," where one guy and one girl actually go out, have fun together, communicate, and get to know one another? It's happening less and less.

And marriage? Many now judge it to be something they can't afford, and the new conventional wisdom seems to be, "Why bother? We'll just cohabitate and maybe consider marriage later, after we are financially secure, after we have a house, after we have had all the adventures we want, and after we are finally willing to settle down and limit our options."

Others think: "Wait for marriage even if you are in love, because marriage and all those commitments might even destroy your love; anyway, marriage is a coin toss, with a 50 percent chance of divorce. So why try it?"

And: "We can't afford kids."

Still, others say: "Why date? Isn't that a throwback to the 1950s? Just get to know someone by hanging out, and if you are attracted to each other, hook up. If it's still going well, move in together and see how that works. Don't give up your options too soon and don't take the risk of actually getting married or having kids—at least not for several years."

Conventional wisdom—where does it come from, and why doesn't it pay more attention to the actual facts?

The problem is that this kind of thinking is based on false paradigms. A solid majority of first marriages do not end in divorce, and it's the very high failure rate of second and third marriages that gets the divorce rate up around 50 percent. And the US Department of Agriculture's estimate that it costs more than $300,000 (inflation adjusted) to raise a child includes assumptions like adding a new room onto your house for each new child. The fact is that kids aren't necessarily as expensive as we are told.

Real, one-on-one dating is the best and most enjoyable way to get to know another person deeply and intimately. And as mentioned, marriages that happen before cohabitation last longer and have a better chance of enduring than those that happen after cohabitation.

Struggling together financially in the early years of marriage is okay. In fact, it's more than okay. Most married couples will tell you that those lean early years were wonderful, at least in retrospect. The idea that you need to own a house with a paid-down mortgage and have high incomes before you can marry or have a child is nonsense. Why not share the challenges of getting established and comfortable rather than each doing it alone? If you are going to be poor for a while, as most of us were, why not be poor with a partner?

And it turns out that marriage is the most exciting option anyway.

Everyone is unique. Everyone needs to find what is best for him or her. There is no pattern or timetable or sequence that works for everyone. But there is danger in listening too much to the current trends and the prevailing wisdom of staying vital and fulfilled by doing your own independent thing and keeping all your self-entertaining options open for as long as you possibly can. Those with that attitude will find that what looked exciting in their twenties will start to look a little stereotyped in their thirties—and may look like an absolute drag in their forties and beyond.

You can keep looking elsewhere for excitement and adventure—trying all kinds of thrill-seeking, from extreme sports to video games to buying a better car or finding a flashier boyfriend or girlfriend. And you can seek peace and contentment in everything from meditation to religion to a new app on deep breathing.

Or you can up the ante, double down, take the biggest risk of all with the biggest potential rewards of excitement, joy, and thrills. And this one, this ultimate and unmatched adventure, is marriage and family.

Of this we are sure: Eli and Charity, our two youngest who have each pretty much maxed out when it comes to excitement, would tell you—unequivocally—that the true adventure of life is total commitment to spouse and family.[6]

6-6: THE ROMANCE OF RESTRAINT

Romance is enhanced by restraint and diluted by philandry.

What comes to mind when you say "romance"? Is it the romantic period of history or the romance of old movies and charming old stories? Or some may say— almost critically or in disbelief—"Wow, that was so romantic" when someone does something rather dramatic or sentimental.

Is romance from another time? And is that why romance novels always seem to have a historical setting?

Has something been lost? Is there still a place for romance in today's world? Can people still be swept away, or is that just a whimsical part of our imaginations?

Do the words of old romantic songs, such as these from "On the Street Where You Live" from Lerner and Loewe's *My Fair Lady*, hold any relevance today?

If you think, as many seem to, that romance is basically a relic or an artifact of an earlier age, and if you wonder whether perhaps we have lost something wonderful, and if you might be interested in recovering some of the old romance in your modern life, then maybe the first place to start is by asking how it was lost.

Could it be that by giving up discipline and restraint and chastity, our society has also been giving up romance?

Has something been lost? Is there still a place for romance in today's world?

Could it be that something as simple as *sequence* has a great deal to do with romance? Consider the sequence of the old nursery rhyme: "First comes love, then comes marriage, then comes the baby in the baby carriage."

Contrast that with this less appealing rhyme that might describe today: "Do what you want, whenever you choose, whatever you gain, whatever you lose."

Or, in a less poetic form, we might describe the mores of today's culture like this:

"First comes sex, which might at some point connect itself to love, and possibly even lead to marriage. Or have a baby sometime if you wish, with or without a partner, and either before or after that elusive thing called love."

Could it be possible that one particular sequence is conducive to romance and many other sequences are not? Might it be that the selfish satisfaction of lust and the desire for instant gratification in everything from love to money are the very things putting real romance out of reach?

Is it possible that physical discipline and sexual restraint, far from being the unhealthy, unnatural suppressants they are often portrayed as being today, are actually the formula for genuine romance?

What is it that is so appealing about an old movie or novel in which people *don't* jump into bed on their first night together—where they take their time, talking and doing things together and falling in love emotionally and mentally before they make love physically? Why do those stories feel so romantic to us?

Maybe all these questions suggest another way of describing the sequence that leads to magical romance: social attraction first, then the mental acquaintance, then the emotional and spiritual compatibility, and then—last instead of first—the physical. Maybe sex is

more romantic when it follows the other four than it is when it pre-
cedes them. Maybe that's why just a touch of the hand or a simple
kiss or embrace can seem so sexy in an old movie. Maybe waiting
really does make it better.

If you have pursued a different, less romantic sequence, it is not
irreversible. There is nothing to stop you from starting over—from
putting the physical on hold for a bit to focus and concentrate for a
while on really knowing and appreciating each other socially, mentally, emotionally, and spiritually.

If you do that, we have two promises for you:

1. Your relationship will be visited with the magic of more
   real romance than you have ever felt.
2. When preceded and enshrouded by romance, the physical
   will be better than it has ever been.

To underscore this whole point, let us share an article written
by our youngest daughter, Charity. We named her Charity partly
because we loved the sound of the word and partly because we loved
what it meant. She got called "Chastity" a lot by mistake.

Charity was a precocious child and a joy to our whole family,
and she grew into an absolutely beautiful and delightful young lady.
She graduated from Wellesley College with honors and studied for a
time in Jerusalem along the way.

She now lives in London with her husband and two little boys,
but when she wrote this, she was single and lived in Palo Alto,
California, working for Clayton Christensen's education think tank.
We love Charity's writing (and find ourselves reading it almost
every day in her blog posts at www.drippingwithpassion.blogspot.
com), so when she said she had a guest column for us, we jumped at
the chance. Here is a portion of Charity's article on chastity:

My favorite part of Victor Hugo's masterpiece *Les Misérables*
(and there are just so many brilliant parts) is the author's
description of the wedding night of lovers Marius and

Cosette. Yes, it's my favorite part. As I read these words, I feel an immense swell of gratitude for the concept of chastity. Quoting from the novel:

> *Here we stop. Upon the threshold of wedding nights stands an angel smiling, his finger on his lip. The soul enters into contemplation before this sanctuary, in which is held the celebration of love.*
>
> *There must be gleams of light above those houses. The joy which they contain must escape in light through the stones of the walls, and shine dimly into the darkness. It is impossible that this sacred festival of destiny should not send a celestial radiation to the infinite. Love is the sublime crucible in which is consummated in the fusion of man and woman; the one being, the triple being, the final being, the human trinity, springs from it. This birth of two souls into one must be an emotion for space. . . . A nuptial bed makes a halo in the darkness. . . . If, at that supreme hour, the wedded pair, bewildered with pleasure, and believing themselves alone, were to listen, they would hear in their chamber a rustling of confused wings.*
>
> *Perfect happiness implies the solidarity of the angels. That little obscure alcove has for its ceiling the whole heavens. When two mouths, made sacred by love, draw near each other to create, it is impossible that above that ineffable kiss there should not be a thrill in the immense mystery of the stars. These are the true felicities. No joy beyond these joys. Love is the only ecstasy, everything else weeps. . . . There is no other pearl to be found in the dark folds of life. To love is a consummation.*

Hugo has me completely convinced: The greatest of mortal happiness is to be found in pure, pure love in which the full physical manifestation has been preserved. There's no way I'm missing that.

Now, I would never dream to impose my belief in abstinence on others, and I fully recognize that many find happiness and healthy relationships without it. I also recognize that love that may seem broken can become pure again.

I am so grateful for an understanding of the principle of chastity in my own life. I am grateful because I know it protects me from so many shades of heartache. But even more so I am grateful because it makes me eligible to experience the greatest of any human joy.

> The greatest of mortal happiness is to be found in pure, pure love in which the full physical manifestation has been preserved. There's no way I'm missing that.

The closest to heaven I've ever felt has been while witnessing marriage ceremonies which, dense and gleaming, are a remarkably strong motivator of restraint. Indeed, watching two faithful people look into each other's glossy eyes and make lasting vows—two people who have sacrificed to give of themselves wholly and purely to each other and none else—is just incredible. I always leave these type of marriage ceremonies with a tear-drenched face, a heart positively bursting with love and joy, and a will fiercely determined to kneel at that altar one day myself, worthy and pure, across from another worthy and pure. It is worth any wait, any struggle, any feat of self-control.

And then, to meet the angels in a wedding night that causes "a thrill in the immense mystery of the stars"—there's no way I'm missing that.[7]

6-7: THERE IS NO ONE-SIZE-FITS-ALL ANSWER

We have a daughter-in-law who marched through the Harvard graduation line during the third trimester of her pregnancy.

She was a huge curiosity (excuse the pun) and made the front page of the Harvard Crimson *newspaper. "Just imagine," the article said, "someone having a child while still in college! Someone who is married while still an undergraduate!"*

It was unheard of. The reporter who wrote the article searched the Harvard rolls and found that there were only twelve married or engaged students in the entire undergraduate student body.

And by the way, this daughter's daughter—our granddaughter—is now applying to Harvard where she hopes to go as a student-athlete swimmer. In her letter to the swimming coach, referring to her in-womb location when her mother graduated, she pointed out that, in a sense, she had already "swum for Harvard."

We hear the questions so often: "Is waiting to marry until you have a job and a house the right thing to do?" Or, "Is marrying early and struggling along together the right thing?" Of course, the answer is that there is no one right way. Everyone has to find what is right for them.

What bugs us is the growing sentiment in favor of waiting, waiting, and waiting, even when two people feel that they have found each other and that they want to share their lives. This may be right for some, but it is certainly not right for all.

We married when Linda had just finished college and Richard was just starting graduate school. The first years were a challenge, to say the least. We had a food budget of twelve dollars a week for the two years we were in Boston and had to spend most of it at the outdoor Haymarket Square vegetable market because that is where we could get the most for our money. Our first child came during those penniless first two years and squeezed our budget even tighter. We drove a fifteen-year-old car (when we had a buck or two for gas) and, as mentioned earlier, our idea of entertainment and recreation was to fly paper airplanes across the Charles River from our balcony with other poor graduate school couples.

But we look back on those "starving" years with relish, and with joy. The struggle and the budgeting and the going without drew our little beginning family together and made us more appreciative of the few little things we were able to have later on.

The fact is that no one ever knows when he or she will meet the right person. Falling in love is not something we can program or time-manage. When it happens, people are not always ready for it. It is not always the best time. It may be a little earlier or a little later in life than what they think of as the ideal.

But when it happens to you and when you know it has happened, why wait? Is it better to struggle together or separately? Are marriage and family really about being comfortable and convenient?

Now lest anyone think we are sanctioning or recommending early marriage or having kids on a whim, let us say that it is wise to be reasonable. Waiting for more maturity or more education or

Waiting longer and longer for more convenience and more comfort is almost always a bad idea.

for parents and families to become better acquainted and to approve of one another—all are almost always good ideas. What we are against is waiting longer and longer for more convenience and more comfort. This is almost always a bad idea. Make deliberate, well-considered decisions based on your mind and your heart—and not on the prevailing trends or public sentiment.

As we write this chapter, our eldest grandson is preparing for his marriage (and "eldest" is an interesting word in this case, because he is only twenty-one and his fiancé just turned twenty). Most would agree that that's early, but several of our children married in their late twenties and one has not yet married because he still has not found "the one"—and many would say that's late. But aren't you glad that every story is different and that there are many "right ways"?

Make your own decisions and push back against some of the "prevailing wisdom"—not only on timing, but on a host of other assumptions:

- You do not always *have* to have two incomes to raise a family.
- It *doesn't* cost a third of a million dollars to raise a child.
- Aggressive, career-oriented persons *can* still prioritize their kids and families.
- And waiting to marry until school is done and financial comfort is achieved is *not* the only wise or prudent way to go.

7. The Equality Myth

(AND OTHER MYTHS AND TRUTHS ABOUT SAMENESS.)

MYTH: Equality should be the prime goal of your relationship or your marriage.

TRUTH: Striving for equality breeds comparing and criticism, and it may produce more competition than compatibility. It is better to work for a marriage of synergistic oneness that breeds cooperation and compensates for one another's weaknesses.

1. SUB-MYTH: You have to be the same to be equal.

   TRUTH: The best kind of equality is oneness, and it thrives on different but equally important roles.

2. SUB-MYTH: The key to a good marriage is for both partners to go 50 percent and meet in the middle.

   TRUTH: You may have to go 90 percent to meet your spouse's 10 percent sometimes, and your partner may have to go 90 percent to meet you other times.

3. SUB-MYTH: Feminism is about eliminating all differences between men and women.

   TRUTH: Feminism is about women and men being different but equal.

7-1: THE COMPLEX QUESTION OF EQUALITY IN MARRIAGE

Richard: I was a student at the Harvard Business School at the height of the most militant period of feminism, a time that woke a lot of people up in a good way, but also a time when the definition of equality and the definition of sameness became a bit mixed and muddled. The women in my class wanted to dress like men, act like men, and essentially be like men.

We had one French guy in our class who begged to differ.

"Vive la différence!" he said. "We should be celebrating the wonderful and mutually attractive differences between real men and real women, not trying to eliminate them!"

Feminism, we think, has grown up since then. Women legitimately want to be equal with men, but not the same as men. Women want to be paid the same, valued the same, and judged the same—but do not want to be exactly alike.

And this is the pattern we should follow in our marriages!

It is proper, of course, and fashionable and certainly politically correct to want and to advocate equality in a marriage relationship. But what does *equality* actually mean? The word seems to have many contexts and definitions. Does it mean sameness? Or can it mean different but equally important roles?

Smart couples enjoy specialization and figure out together who is best at what, and then manage their marriage and family accordingly.

In a company, can a vice president of marketing be equal to a vice president of production? Can two people be equal when they possess different gifts, different interests, different methods, and very different ways of doing things?

Any man who thinks he should have power or dominance over his wife is missing the whole point of marriage. And any woman who thinks that she has to do exactly the same things as her husband to be equal to him is also missing the point.

Marriage is about synergy and synchronicity and even symbiosis. It is about making each other better and making each other happier. It is more about always making up than about never disagreeing, and it is more about learning together and from each other than about who can win.

Perhaps the most profound and unassailable definition of equality applies to two indispensable and complementing parts of one whole.

Are the sails and the hull of a schooner equal? They are certainly equally essential though one is in the air and one is in the water, one is made of canvas and the other of metal, and one is visible while the other is hidden.

Smart couples enjoy specialization and figure out together who is best at what, and then manage their marriage and family accordingly.

Men generally have propensities in some things and women in others, but there are endless exceptions and cases where those propensities are opposite or mixed. There is no one-size-fits-all and no one definition of equality and oneness.

And since this is a book about all phases of marriage, from newly wed to nearly dead, it should also be mentioned that as time passes and capacities wax and wane, there may have to be shifts in who does what and in how much each can do.

Wise couples think about, analyze, and seek to work out and learn from their differences rather than eliminating them.

So, if we are going to strive for equality, may we at least look for a type of equality that is symbiotic and synergistic, where two parts of a whole depend on each other, support each other, and make each other better—where the whole is greater (and happier) than the sum of its parts!

7-2: THE PROBLEM WITH EQUALITY

(AND THE BETTER PARADIGM OF ONENESS.)

In our own marriage we dumped the "equality" goal, which meant slowing one of us down so the other could catch up. It was unnatural. Unity was a better goal, allowing us to celebrate our differences in aptitudes and attitudes while blending and converging on our goals and priorities.

But we knew that there was a step beyond unity, an ideal to strive for that is higher and vastly more synergistic, and we came to call it "oneness." Oneness, as we define it herein, is a change not in degree but in kind. It is a paradigm shift wherein, without minimizing (in fact maximizing) our individuality, we become two parts of one greater whole and where that new, combined entity becomes not only more important than either part, but more than the sum of its parts.

We give equality a lot of lip service and praise, but when applied to marriage, the concept has problems. Insisting on equality can be like trying to make every game end in a tie. If we are constantly worrying about equality then somebody is always a little ahead or a little behind and we have to keep compensating and adjusting. Marriage is not about keeping score.

There is an element of competition in equality, and a certain amount of comparing and judging.

Maybe the best marriages are not about equality. Maybe they are about *oneness*.

In our definition, oneness brings two halves together in a merger that allows for synergy, for specialization, for different

There is an element of competition in equality, and a certain amount of comparing and judging.

abilities and skills, and for mutual appreciation rather than mutual competition.

When we got married, we had the thought that Linda, the violinist, would teach Richard to play the cello and that Richard, the tennis player, would groom Linda for mixed doubles.

Neither worked out very well.

Today, Richard can manage the eight notes required for the cello part of Pachelbel's Cannon in D, and Linda can get a slow serve in and then move off the court to let Richard play the point.

Not exactly what either of us had in mind. But some serendipity happened along the way: Linda became an avid tennis fan, and Richard now adores classical symphonic music.

"If you can't do it, appreciate it," has become our motto. Linda doesn't have to drag Richard to the symphony—we drag each other!

We are actually writing this chapter from Roland-Garros, site of the great French Open tennis tournament in Paris where Linda is at least as into it as Richard. ("It's not just the tennis, it's the food," she says.) Whenever we get a speaking invitation in Europe in the late spring, we build Roland-Garros or Wimbledon into our schedule; not to mention Sir Neville Marriner (and now his replacement) and the orchestra at St.-Martin-in-the-Fields.

So the marriage message here is simple: Adopt each other's interests and passions, whatever they are.

One of our daughters has adopted her husband's love for camping. Another daughter has discovered that if she reads parts of the *Economist* every week, which her husband reads cover to cover, the two of them will have a lot more to talk about. One of our sons is working hard to learn another language because his Swiss wife happens to speak seven of them and because they now live in Zurich.

> **Let's look for a non-sameness kind of equality that we can rename "oneness" and that celebrates our differences and welds them into one greater whole.**

Now, you may not get much chance to completely devote yourself to any of your spouse's passions, or to your own for that matter, while the kids are around. (Or, better said, the kids had better be your main interest or passion while they are at home.) But remember, the empty nest is coming sometime, and if you have learned to love what each other loves then it will be a happier nest!

For us, a lot is tied to a little saying we have come to love: "If it's important to you, it's important to me."

You can live on borrowed light or borrowed passion for something for a while, and then—whaddaya know—you start loving it like your partner loves it.

Let's look for a non-sameness kind of equality that we can rename "oneness" and that celebrates our differences and welds them into one greater whole. Let's learn from each other's skills and interests! Let's learn the marvelous marriage synergy of accepting each other's passions, then adopting and loving them.

Theoretical equality feels like a race and requires constant analysis and readjustment—and there is always the worry of who is ahead. A tag team race, with you both on the same side, is both better and faster.

We have eight married children, and each of their marriages is unique. As we observe them and watch these couples grow together—through thick and thin, through good times and hard times—we are amazed at the resilience of marriage and impressed by their various ways of blending their differences into oneness.

Actually, on the various parts of a good oneness marriage, elective, chosen, deliberate *inequality* can be a good thing—with one partner taking the lead in some things and doing less on others and vice versa, depending on aptitudes and interests and circumstances. Good marriages are better described as finding oneness of purpose and strategic teamwork than simply as equality. The oneness we should strive for is not sameness but synergy, not equality but equanimity, not a cloning but a combining.

Are the two wheels of a bicycle equal or do they each do different things that make up one functional bike? Oneness is a happier, stronger, and simpler thing than equality. And oneness isn't one easy, one-size-fits-all formula. It is something hard-won over a lot of years and after overcoming a lot of difficulties and hard times.

7-3: TRUE VS. FALSE FEMINISM

Three of our daughters did their undergraduate degrees at Wellesley College, a truly wonderful all-women liberal arts college near Boston. We love almost everything about Wellesley, from the rigorous academics and small, intimate classes taught by full professors to the gorgeous wooded campus complete with its own lake.

You might wonder about the social life at an all-women's college, but students cross-register with MIT and interact with all the other great universities in the Boston area. Wellesley happens to be Hillary Clinton and Madeleine Albright's alma mater. It is also a very liberal environment and a historic and perennial leader in the feminist movement.

Which brings us to our point: We love feminism when it is defined by and devoted to the true celebration of womanhood and to the worthy goal of complete equality with men. We don't like feminism nearly as much when it goes in the opposite direction—advocating gender irrelevance, complaining that things that are different cannot be equal, and essentially saying that the only relevant and powerful roles are those traditionally held by men.

We think that this kind of negative, skewed, and extremist thinking about gender stems from the mis-definition of equality as sameness. And when we fall into that trap—thinking that unless two things are exactly the same they cannot be equal—the world becomes a confusing place.

Would we really benefit by having a bunch of cars around with two engines and no transmission?

Think it through one more time: At a college, can a professor of chemistry be equal with a professor of English literature in pay, in importance, and in recognition? Of course. Can the first violinist in an orchestra be equal to a first clarinetist? Yes.

Are they the same? No.

What if the transmission of a car insisted on being the engine, or vice versa? Would we really benefit by having a bunch of cars around with two engines and no transmission?

Who's to say whether the engine or the transmission is more important? Perhaps making the car *go* is the objective—maximizing its ability to get somewhere. And maybe it is the car and its destination that matter more than its individual parts.

And maybe, in life, having a responsible, contributing household is the goal—maximizing the chance of children growing strong and productive. And maybe it is the family that matters most and that can make the most progress and register the most joy—when spouses work together, we can have more joy, both as individuals and as partners.

In Chapter 7-1, we mentioned my French classmate who sought to redefine feminism as an appreciation and celebration of differences rather than a quest for sameness. I still vividly remember the day when, after every discussion seemed to turn into a question of gender equality, he bounded to the front of the classroom and delivered his passionate oration on "Vive la différence." Of course, he said, there should be equality of pay and of opportunity, but, he urged he urged his classmates, "Let women be women—real, strong women, and let men be men. Appreciate the differences; appreciate the beauty and power of gender. Revel in it. Understand that it is what makes the world go round."

We need to celebrate womanhood and manhood and glory in their difference—while at the same time insisting on their equal value and overall equality.

7-4: STRIVING FOR THE ONENESS LEVEL OF MARRIAGE

Only one thing is better than synergy, and that is oneness.

Marriage can exist on at least five levels, and it can progress from one level to the next and to the next. Let us try to name these levels and describe them briefly and then suggest the possibility of climbing the ladder of love.

Level one is a marriage of convenience. Two people think they are in love, so they decide to live together—with or without an actual ceremony.

Level two is a marriage of contract. Husband and wife get married legally—often religiously—and make at least a pledge of "in sickness and in health" and "till death do us part."

Level three is a marriage of true commitment. Beyond the formality of a wedding, both parties exclusively and completely commit themselves to each other and give and receive the security of knowing that there will never be any other.

Level four is a marriage of synergy. This occurs when the man and the woman, the yin and the yang, learn to complement and complete each other so efficiently that the total is greater than the sum of its parts.

Level five is a marriage of oneness in which the commitment and the synergy continue to grow to the point where the couple shares everything and where their oneness becomes an entity that supersedes their individualness. Everything they seek, they seek together, and they are essentially fused into something that swallows up even as it preserves their separate gifts and natures.

Everything they seek, they seek together, and they are essentially fused into something that swallows up even as it preserves their separate gifts and natures.

Whatever level you perceive yourself to be on, you can progress to the next one if you both want to. Decide together on a collective gift from yourselves to yourselves. Give the gift of a mutual commitment to go from whatever level you are on to the next level. And use this book and any other resources you can find to help you get there.

> *As you know by now, we've always liked the word* synergy. *It is a dynamic word, sounding a little like energy, and it has an almost magical meaning that we have referred to repeatedly throughout the book: a combination where "the whole is greater than the sum of its parts"—one plus one equaling three, five, or more.*

The word comes from the Greek word *synergia,* meaning "working together."

We hear the term used most often in business, but its most artful and appropriate application is in marriage. It's a wonderful thing to see a married couple where the husband and the wife have different personalities, different skills, and different approaches that complement and enhance each other.

One way to develop marital synergy, and to dissipate conflict and minimize disagreement, is to have a private, weekly "feelings session"—or Executive Session—where the two of you, in a respectful if not spiritual environment, each take a few minutes to share your feelings with each other. Start with the positive, but also share any moments when you felt misunderstood or disrespected during the past week and take the opportunity to apologize for any hurt you may have caused. Talk about your love and your beliefs and share your heart.

Marriage can become a genuinely synergistic relationship where the developing oneness of the two of you never robs your individuality and yet becomes greater than your sum, and eventually creates a combined entity that is more capable, more joyful, and more conducive to growth than either by itself.

7-5: SPIRITUAL DERIVATIVES OF ONENESS IN MARRIAGE

In the earlier parts of our speaking and writing career, particularly when we were with very diverse audiences in various parts of the world, we were very careful not to mention or reference anything too religious or spiritual for fear of offending someone. As time has gone by, however, we have become more and more candid about our own beliefs and less and less likely to exclude spiritual aspects of what we are saying or writing. And occasionally we do offend someone who will come up after a speech and say something like, "I didn't pay to come here and have you preach to me." But for every one like that, there are at least ten who say something like, "That was the point where you really reached me—when you got to the spiritual."

Contemplate for a moment the spiritual idealism and definitions of oneness:

Asian religion and philosophy call it the yin and the yang, the two great opposites that hold the universe in check. The light and the dark, the low and the high, the hot and the cold, the male and the female. Yin and yang are seemingly contrary forces that are interconnected and interdependent in the natural world, and that give rise to each other in turn—complementary opposites that interact within a greater whole, as part of a dynamic system.

In Chinese thought, there is a deeply spiritual aspect to yin and yang, even to the point of the earth's creation and operation. And it is only with both the yin and yang, with their combination, that a complete wholeness is achieved.

> **Virtually all of the world's major religions teach that a man and woman enhance and complete each other.**

And so it is with a man and woman in marriage. The two complement, compensate, create, and complete each other. Separately they cannot long exist, at least not in their intended, ideal form.

In the Judeo-Christian tradition, Eve and Adam were made as companions and partners, completing elements of each other. And it was Eve who figured out the need to fall into mortality.

In different language but with similar meaning, virtually all of the world's major religions teach that a man and woman enhance and complete each other and that an individual man or woman is a partial rather than a total and perfectible entity.

Once again, the goal of a marriage is not sameness or interchangeability between husband and wife but rather a dynamic interplay of opposites or differentness that produces a whole that is greater than the sum of its parts. In our marriages, we should be grateful rather than resentful of differences and seek to merge them effectively rather than eliminate them.

The merging will take some rigorous stirring and will sometimes produce some explosive interaction, but if we concentrate on the goal of improving oneness rather than on selfish wants, something greater will emerge.

The Bible teaches that man should "leave his father and mother and cleave unto his wife and they shall be one flesh,"[1] and Jesus said that "what God hath joined together, let no man tear asunder."[2]

The Apostle Paul said, "Neither is the man without the woman neither the woman without the man in the Lord."[3]

Some claim that Christ de-prioritized marriage and family by saying things such as, "He that loveth father or mother [or son or daughter] more than me is not worthy of me."[4]

The other interpretation of that (and our interpretation) is that Jesus was magnifying the importance and preeminence of family and of marriage by making it the ultimate comparison and essentially saying that the only thing on earth more important than family is a direct call from God himself.

According to a Wikipedia entry on Christian views of marriage, "Jesus used the image of marriage and the family to teach the basics about the kingdom of God. He inaugurated his ministry by blessing the wedding feast at Cana."[5] Even Christ's reference to himself as a bridegroom suggests the emphasis and priority he placed on marriage.

The teachings of Christ and of his apostles leave little question about the powerful preeminence of marriage in a positive and fulfilling Christian life.

Paul said "marriage is honorable in all" and suggested that husbands should love their wives as they love their own bodies.[6]

Christianity, as well as other world religions through the ages, has been the staunchest advocate, practitioner, and defender of marriage on earth. According to Wikipedia, "Christians typically regard marriage as instituted and ordained by God for the lifelong relationship between one man as husband and one woman as wife."[7]

Bottom line: the general case for marriage is strong, and the spiritual case for marriage is even stronger.

7-7: THE ETERNAL ONENESS OF MARRIAGE

We have traveled to more than one hundred countries and presented or lectured in more than fifty, usually on marriage and family themes, and if we were to synthesize the spiritual sentiments we have heard from people all over the world into one sentence, it might read like this: "Heaven would not be heaven without my spouse and children being with me."

Whether Hindu, Buddhist, Jew, Muslim, a member of a Christian faith, or those who say they are spiritual but not religious, we have heard individuals all around the world express their own personal faith that the bonds of marriage and family must somehow be able to endure beyond death. It is just the natural thing to believe. And while many theologies may argue to the contrary, it will continue to be a part of the conviction of all those who love their family deeply and cannot conceive of any sort of paradise without them.

Our own personal faith may go beyond the still-together hope, because it includes five beliefs that might be thought of by many as radical:

1. That neither an individual man nor an individual woman is a perfectible entity and that if one is to pursue, over eternity, Christ's admonition to "be ye therefore perfect," he

will have to do it via the oneness of marriage—joining the yin and the yang or the masculine and the feminine into a synergistic whole that can potentially and ultimately possess attributes and capabilities that are otherwise impossible. Thus, the goal of marriage is not for two persons to become alike, but to combine their individual qualities into a greater and more complete oneness.

2. That those who do not have the opportunity for marriage and children on this earth will have those options in the spirit world to follow.

3. That individuals on this earth have more power and control over the happiness of their spouse than they do over their own.

4. That in matters relating to their own families, marriage partners have the access and the right to direct guidance and inspiration from God, unfiltered by ecclesiastical leaders.

5. That it is the family, not a church or any religious institution, that goes on through eternity—and that churches or mosques or synagogues or any other faith-based support mechanism is, in essence, the spiritual scaffolding with which we build lasting families.

We believe that we are not physical beings who occasionally have a spiritual experience, but we are spiritual beings having a physical experience—one of the purposes of which is to form families that will endure beyond the grave and in fact outlast all other earthly institutions.

In this paradigm, marriage is not only the natural and desired state for men and women, it is the eternal state by which divine purposes are fulfilled and through which each of us can evolve and progress. And in this context, the highest and most valuable thing to work on in life is a oneness in marriage.

8. The Myth of Marriage's Demise

(AND OTHER MYTHS AND TRUTHS ABOUT THE MACRO OF MARRIAGE IN SOCIETY.)

MYTH: Marriage is on the decline and disappearing as an institution.

TRUTH: The strongest, most fulfilling marriages in the history of the world exist today.

1. **SUB-MYTH: Educated people are not getting married.**

   TRUTH: Today, it is college educated people, more than any other demographic, that are getting married and staying married.

2. **SUB-MYTH: Most people in today's world no longer want to get married or be married.**

   TRUTH: Polls show that over 90 percent of people want to be married.

3. **SUB-MYTH: Marriage is simply not as relevant or as useful as it once was in society.**

   TRUTH: Given the disconnected, polarizing, fracturing, temporary, and transient nature of today's culture, the bonds and connections and commitments of marriage have never been more important and more needed.

8-1: DISCOURAGING STATISTICS, WONDERFUL EXCEPTIONS, AND A NEW TREND

Our personal mission statement for our writing and speaking and social media related to families is "fortify families by celebrating commitment, popularizing parenting, and validating values."

We think that more *celebrating commitment* or being positive about the beauty and benefits of marriage can ultimately save and elevate this oldest institution in the world, and we all ought to join together in that celebration and promotion!

As a reader, you might say, "Working on my own marriage is hard enough—why should I pay any attention to the broader trends and public opinion polls about marriage across the world?"

The answer is that we are all affected by trends and polls and what others are doing, and if we believe the myths about the demise of marriage, it is likely to affect at least our optimism and hopes for the world and will perhaps also discourage us or dampen our belief that our own marriages can survive and thrive. So we need to believe! *Believe* not only in your own marriage but in the institution of marriage—the oldest and most important institution in the world, the greatest protector of children, and the most basic unit of society.

Yes, there are some negative trends; the marriage rate is dropping and most young couples who move in together today are cohabitating, unmarried. But on the other hand, most of them see the very act of living together as the beginning of commitment and say that they want to and plan to get married.

Yes, there are polls that indicate less and less interest in marriage among the general population. But on the other hand, there are also polls that indicate that virtually everyone sees marriage as the ideal and hopes for it sometime during their life.

Yes, there are many who think both marriage and children are luxuries that they can't afford. But on the other hand, there are more and more who believe that financial struggles can be shared within a marriage and who don't buy into the inflated estimates of how much it costs to raise a child.

Yes, chosen singleness and living alone is a popular trend right now, particularly in many large cities. But on the other hand, people are finding it less free and less fulfilling than they thought it would be, realizing their need for someone.

Yes, independence and keeping all options open are mantras of the millennial generation. But on the other hand, like all trends, its downsides and loneliness are being exposed, and the interdependence of marriage partnerships are starting to look better and better.

Yes, more and more less educated and low- and middle-income segments of the population seem to be rejecting marriage. But on the other hand, more and more college educated and higher-income folks are embracing marriage like never before and have simply decided that "married with kids" is the best and happiest way to live.

The prediction of the demise of marriage is premature and ultimately false.

So, yes, the numbers indicate that the institution of marriage is in trouble. But there is a powerful and influential counter trend—the quality and satisfaction of marriage, within the sectors that embrace it, has never been higher.

We need to look at both sides of this teeter-totter—both the general decline and the specific upswing and improvement.

As we look deeper into both the dark side of declining marriage and the light side of its new popularity, we think you will conclude, as we have, that the prediction of the demise of marriage is premature and ultimately false.

In his book *The All-or-Nothing Marriage,* author Eli J. Finkel, after an exhaustive study of marriage in America today, says this, "It's true that the institution of marriage in America is struggling. But I came to realize that the best marriages today are better than the best marriages of earlier eras; indeed, they are the best marriages that the world has ever known."[1]

So, whatever you see or think or observe about marriage in general, remember this: You and your spouse are the determiners of what your marriage is and will be, irrespective of what is going on around you, and you have more power and more opportunity today than ever before to achieve a truly great marriage. You can learn from each other, you can grow, you can be more deliberate and strategic, and you can gradually and steadily improve your marriaging.

8-2: MARRIAGE TODAY:
THE DARK SIDE

If we only look at the numbers—the statistics and trends and polls—the future of marriage looks pretty dark indeed.

Despite the optimism of the last chapter, this Myth #8—the demise of marriage—can seem not only accurate but irrefutable if you look at certain statistics and public opinion polls.

Marriage is getting hit hard from all sides. On one side, divorce rates continue at a high level; on another side, marriage rates keep falling as more people choose to stay single. On the third side, cohabitation replaces marriage for more than two-thirds of couples.

Taken together, these attacks are striking a devastating blow and have brought us to a point where less than half of all adults will be married and less than one-fourth of teenaged children will live in a home with both of their parents.

The results may be catastrophic!

Theoretically, a commune can raise children, or a welfare system, or an orphanage—even a prison can do the job. But none of them do it as well as the family and all of them are impossibly expensive to the society that surrounds them.

Married, committed parents do the job best and do it by far the most economically.

A generation ago, no one would have questioned the premise that the family is the basic unit of society. Today, it is questioned from many sides. In his ominously titled landmark work *The Rise of Post-familialism: Humanity's Future?*, demographer Joel Kotkin says:

A generation ago, no one would have questioned the premise that the family is the basic unit of society.

> Today, in the high-income world and even in some developing countries, there is a shift to a new social model. Increasingly, family no longer serves as the central, organizing feature of society . . . [and] as Austrian demographer Wolfgang Lutz has pointed out, the shift to an increasingly childless society creates "self-reinforcing mechanisms" that make childlessness, singleness, or one-child families increasingly prominent.[2]

Kotkin points out the ramifications of this shift, some of them political:

> A society that is increasingly single and childless is likely to be more concerned with serving current needs than addressing the future-oriented requirements of children. Since older people vote more than younger ones and children have no say at all, political power could shift toward non-childbearing people.

Statistically, we have generally been moving away from the married-with-kids model for some time, and that movement away has picked up momentum in the last decade.

As David Brooks of the *New York Times* pointed out:

In a 2011 survey, a majority of Taiwanese women under fifty said they did not want children. Fertility rates in Brazil have dropped from 4.3 babies per woman thirty-five years ago to 1.9 babies today. These are all stunningly fast cultural and demographic shifts. The entire developed world is moving in the same basic direction, from societies oriented around the two-parent family to cafeteria societies with many options.[3]

Where is it all going? Is marriage obsolete? Are those of us who participate in it just trying to resuscitate and breathe life into an institution that is doomed to die?

8-3: MARRIAGE TODAY: THE BRIGHT SIDE

We once spoke at a marriage conference where the prevailing opinion was that marriage in an endangered institution on its last leg and was soon to disappear from the earth all together. Some of the speakers with this pessimistic attitude presented compelling statistics to back up their view.

We decided to go the opposite direction in our presentation. We made the case that while there are a lot of things to worry about concerning marriage, the fact is that today, when marriages are good, they are very, very good—better in fact than marriages of any other age in history. And we used personal examples and observations rather than statistics to make our point.

As mentioned, we are all influenced by what we think is going on in society around us. Our view of the macro can influence our hope for the micro. If we think the institution of marriage is doomed, it can make us less hopeful and optimistic about our own marriages. But if we believe that marriage is flourishing and that truly great marriages are possible today, we become more excited about the upside possibilities for our own individual marriage.

They have concluded that "married with children" is the most fulfilling and joyful way to live their lives.

Surveys show that the fastest growing segment of society that embraces marriage is not the religious sector as it once was (although most religions continue to have a pro-marriage effect on their adherents). The demographic group most likely to marry and stay married today are educated, upwardly mobile adults. They are not marrying or staying married because their faith tells them it is the right thing to do (although some are certainly influenced by this); they are doing it because they have concluded that "married with children" is the most fulfilling and joyful way to live their lives.

And the reason this is such a hopeful sign is that this is exactly the demographic that usually sets and leads new trends.

There is no question about the general drift away from marriage, but let's focus on this countertrend going on within a particular demographic where both the quantity and the quality of marriages are on the upswing. And let us tell you about it through our own experience:

One of our main speaking clients over the past couple of decades has been the Young Presidents' Organization (YPO), a worldwide association of corporate presidents and CEOs. To join, you must head a multimillion-dollar company before you turn forty. Thus, by definition, these are young, educated, aggressive, type-A personalities who want to be the best at everything they do, including their parenting and their marriaging. They are, in a way, the prototype of a new kind of marriage and parenting and a new kind of family that combines the best from the traditional strong-commitment marriages of the past and the equal-partnership, role-sharing marriages most aspire to.

YPOers—as evidenced by how often they bring us in to speak to them in their various chapters around the world—are very, very interested in developing strong and lasting marriages and families and in raising responsible and highly motivated kids.

Their divorce rate is low, and their kids are—generally speaking—solid, polite, and high-achieving. These parents prioritize their families and devote a lot of time and mental effort to their marriage relationships and to their parenting.

And while we can't take much credit for any of it, most of them are poster families for the mission statement of our writing and speaking company mentioned earlier: *Fortify families by celebrating commitment, popularizing parenting, bolstering balance, and validating values.*

Curiously, what is happening in the world today is that highly educated and economically successful families are prioritizing and committing themselves to marriage and parenting with

Fathers in this new model of marriage spend much more time with their children and are much more likely to share household duties with their wives.

much more regularity and dedication than lower-income, less-educated parents. Frankly, hands-on parenting and real partnership in marriaging is becoming the thing to do among young, upwardly mobile couples.

According to Richard Reeves's words in *The Atlantic*, "a new version [of marriage] is emerging—egalitarian, committed, and focused on children. There was a time when college-educated women were the least likely to be married. Today they are the most important drivers of the new marriage model. . . . Their marriages offer more satisfaction, last longer and produce more successful children." Reeves goes on to write, "Against all predictions, educated Americans are rejuvenating marriage."[4]

Fathers in this new model of marriage spend much more time with their children and are much more likely to share household duties with their wives. And the great thing about it, at least from our observation, is that these committed, aspiring families are not doing it out of duty but out of joy. They are working at their relationships because they have concluded that relationships are what matter and what will make them happy.

A recent study from the National Marriage Project at the University of Virginia comes to one rather surprising but very strong and well-supported conclusion. It is that "the more educated people are, the better chance they have of getting married and staying married."[5]

And as mentioned, the demographic we are talking about here—the college-educated, higher-income segment of society—is the one that sets patterns and starts trends that are then followed by more and more of the population. We can all hope that this will be the case with more lasting and celebrated commitments, more conscientious marriaging, and more popular and energetic parenting.

8-4: WHERE IS THE MIDDLE OF SOCIETY, AND HOW DO WE CHANGE THE TRENDS?

After looking at the top and bottom echelons of American society, we need to pay attention to the vast middle—because that is where the most people are.

The National Marriage Project, just mentioned in the previous chapter, points out that highly educated people are getting married and staying married, but it then moves on to a much more troublesome conclusion: that moderately educated couples, even those with some college under their belts, are *increasingly* less likely than college grads to get married and to stay married.

In the study, the core conclusion is as follows:

The most consequential marriage trend of our time concerns the broad center of our society, where marriage, that iconic middle-class institution, is foundering. . . .

For the last few decades, the retreat from marriage has been regarded largely as a problem afflicting the poor. But today, it is spreading into the solid middle of the middle class. These are people who work. They pay taxes. They raise children. They take family vacations. But there is one thing that today's moderately educated men and women, unlike

today's college graduates or yesterday's high-school graduates, are increasingly less likely to do: get and stay happily
married. And this is a group that represents 58 percent of
our population.

Thus, there is a growing "marriage gap" between moderately and
highly educated America.

According to the study, this "marginalization of marriage in
Middle America is especially worrisome, because this institution has
long served the American experiment in democracy as an engine of
the American Dream, a seedbed of virtue for children, and one of
the few sources of social solidarity."[6]

The study certainly does not always prove cause and effect, and
of course there are huge numbers of moms and dads who did not
complete college degrees and have wonderful marriages and excep-
tional kids.

But statistically, in the last four decades, moderately educated
Americans have seen their family lives begin to look more and more
like those of the least-educated Americans.

Here are the areas or statistical categories where there have been
steep increases among moderately educated Americans and stability
or decreases among those with college degrees:

- Divorce or separation within ten years of marriage
- Percentage of births to never-married women
- Percentage of women who have had three or more sex
  partners
- Percentage of marrieds who have had sex with someone
  other than their spouse
- Percentage of men unemployed at some point in last ten
  years

And here are the categories where there are big decreases among
the moderately educated and stability or increases among the better
educated:

- Those saying they have a "very happy marriage"
- Percentage of intact first marriages
- Percentage of kids living with both parents
- Percentage believing that premarital sex is always wrong
- Percentage who attend church regularly

The study concludes with this chilling sentence: "It is one of the great social tragedies of our time that marriage is flourishing among the most advantaged and self-actualized groups in our society and waning among those who could most benefit from its economic and child-rearing advantages."

The same trends are illustrated in marriage and family studies from the Pew Research Center which shows a very recent and very pronounced shift from the historical norm of less-educated Americans being more church and family oriented than their more-educated counterparts. The Pew study shows 64 percent of college graduates are currently married, while only 48 percent of high school grads (who have not graduated from college) are married. Additionally, the study found:

> Among the 58 percent of Americans who have high school degrees but no college degrees (a group referred to by the study as "middle Americans"), divorce and co-habitation are up, as are premarital sex and births to teenage moms—while marriage, church attendance, and employment are down. Among more educated Americans, the trends are reversed.[7]

Other related studies show that those who never marry, or those who divorce and don't remarry, do significantly worse financially and have a 75 percent wealth reduction compared to married individuals.

The interesting question related to these studies is this: What are the causes and what are the effects?

We are dealing with four elements here:

1. Education

2. Faith and religion
3. Economics and wealth
4. Marriage and family

There is a tendency to view the world in economic models, so you might say, "A bad economy and high employment cause less education, and both lead to less marriage and family know-how and a departure from faith."

But wouldn't it be equally logical to say, "Those with less education have a harder time getting good jobs and supporting families or living a traditional or religious life."

And religionists might argue well by saying, "Faith and church activity teach family morals and ideals, which include education and lead to economic stability."

There is validity and truth in all of these statements, but none of them is as cause-and-effect logical as a statement suggesting the family as the basic bond and unit of society, of the economy, of religion, and of education: *Stable families and committed marriages provide the environment most conducive to educational achievement, to economic success, and to religious faith for those who desire it.*

Bottom line: The starting place for better education, better faith, and a better economy is better families.

The biggest problem and the prime driver of other problems in middle America is the breakdown of marriage commitment and of stable and prioritized families. Kids growing up in fractured or nonexistent families have a smaller chance of staying in school, a smaller chance of having and holding a job, and fewer role models and lifestyle models that center on church and community. Bottom line: The starting place for better education, better faith, and a better economy is better families.

8-5: HOW WE GOT HERE

A BRIEF HISTORY OF THE DECLINE AND RESURGENCE OF MARRIAGE.

S tarting in the infamous '60s, certain parts of the hippie culture and the intellectual establishment began their chorus against marriage. The mantra was that traditional marriage subjugated and demeaned women and promoted an unequal and patriarchal society.

Furthermore, as the chorus continued into the '70s and '80s, marriage was portrayed as an old-fashioned and outdated institution. Who needs a ceremony and a certificate to love each other or to have children? And who says "first comes love, then comes marriage, then comes the baby in the baby carriage"? Why can't we have those three things in any order we want, and why even bother with the marriage part at all?

Marriage was for dummies, for non-thinkers, and for folks that were so traditional that they just couldn't think of anything to do other than what their parents and grandparents did.

And guess what? As the years passed, more and more people believed the chorus and started singing along. Sometimes the media led the choir. Marriage rates plummeted; cohabitation rates soared. And quickly increasing percentages decided they didn't need either—that staying single and living alone was the way to have real freedom and individual rights and keep all your options open.

Countries that once worried about population control are now panicked by their less-than-replacement birthrates.

The marriage nay-sayers were winning—big time! The statistics and trends proved it.

In the midst of these declining views on marriage there is one group that has fought tirelessly to be granted the right to marry. In 2015, the US Supreme Court granted same-sex couples the right to marry. Some wonder why, when many are so casual about the importance of marriage, there is a group that has worked for years because they wanted marriage rights. Now the highest court in the land has decided that marriage is a very important institution, an honor, a privilege so dear and so relevant that it should not be denied or withheld from anyone.

Whatever one's personal or religious views on marriage, it now seems that we live in a world where the LGBT community desires, values, and demands marriage, while others in society dismiss marriage as unimportant, untimely, and inconvenient.

This shift should motivate us all, straight and gay, to fight even harder to re-enshrine marriage and to promote committed partnerships as the most fulfilling way of life. Even for those who do not equate marriage with morality, there are good reasons, both economic and emotional, to fight hard against the continuing decline of marriage.

Perhaps the most obvious of these is the simple fact that societies with a declining number of marriages and with birthrates that fail to adequately replace one generation with another inevitably face a skewed dependency ratio where ever fewer active workers support more and more retirees. The result is an inverted pyramid of aging people supported by a dwindling number of younger people.

Governments in countries that once worried about population control are now panicked by their less-than-replacement birthrates, and countries ranging from Russia to France to Singapore now offer cash premiums for babies—even bonuses that jump substantially upward for the third and fourth child—and offer more and more liberal maternity and paternity leaves and benefits to encourage more procreation.

> *On a recent speaking trip to Singapore, our host was kidding us good naturedly about the large size of our family. Later, as he was telling us about the cash bonuses that women there receive for having babies, he said "Wow, you should have come here to Singapore to have all of your children! You would be rich!"*

In the United States, people over sixty-five represented 9 percent of the total population in 1960; they represent 16 percent today, and are predicted to represent 25 percent of the population in 2030—corresponding with a steep decline in the number of younger workers. And people over sixty-five receive seven times more in federal spending than children under eighteen.[8]

Anyone hoping for a strong economy must pay attention to studies that consistently show that married adults with children do better in terms of their incomes, their savings, and their preparation for retirement than their single counterparts. After all, the term "economics" is taken from the Greek *oikos* for "home," and *nomia* for "management." As economist Nick Schulz says in his aptly titled book *Home Economics*, "The collapse of the intact family is one of the most significant economic facts of our time."[9]

> *We have been trying, in recent years, to work with national political leaders on the idea of establishing a cabinet level office for parents and children in the Federal Government to monitor and seek ways to support and strengthen families in the American society—because we believe that the way to strengthen this country's economy, its productivity, and its whole society is to help, promote, and fortify its families.*

8-6: IMPORTANCE OF THE INSTITUTION

WHY WE ARE ALL DEPENDENT ON MARRIAGE.

Marriage is a little like air. It's been here forever and we tend to take it for granted.

If air were disappearing, since we are all totally dependent on it, we would be alarmed enough to do everything we could to remedy the situation. Well, marriage is disappearing, and we are all totally dependent on it—yet we are not nearly alarmed enough, and we are doing little to remedy the situation.

The difference, of course, is that the effects on the human body of not having enough air are both immediate and devastating, while the effects on the human race of not having enough marriage take longer to devastate and longer to recognize—but they are no less deadly.

Because we are so used to marriage, we take it for granted as a part of our society and fail to realize that it is more than just a part, it is the foundation. Marriage is what creates the smallest and most basic economic engines that make up our communities and raise the responsible citizens, wage earners, and tax payers of our future. Without the commitment of marriage, these little household units are unstable and largely unreliable, and our whole society moves inexorably toward ever greater moral and economic decline.

This is a book on the "micro" of individual marriages and how to make them better. But our lives unfold within a society where the "macro" of marriage

If marriage goes down, what else goes down with it?

within society affects us all. Everyone has a stake in what is happening to the institution of marriage, and what *will* happen because the state of marriage is indivisibly connected to the state of society.

And we all have to ask the macro question: If marriage goes down, what else goes down with it?

Recently, the *NBC Nightly News* reported that, for the first time in history, there are more adults in the United States who are single than who are married. Economists were quoted saying this is a significant development because of its implications: "More renters than buyers, fewer children, and vastly different spending habits."[10]

Well, guess what? Having fewer married adults will change a lot more in this country than our spending habits. The trend toward chosen singleness and chosen childlessness will change the very fiber of our society.

Let us suggest five sweeping consequences of a continuing trend away from marriage:

1. It will dramatically reduce our economic security.

Families are not only the places where parents nurture and raise children; they are places where people take care of each other and where grown children care for aging parents and grandparents. As longevity increases, there are more and more elderly folks who need some assistance. The worst possible demographic combination is more and more old people and fewer and fewer young people to care for them. The inevitable economic result of increasing singles and decreasing marrieds is the inverted pyramid, where a smaller and smaller workforce has to pay the taxes required to support a larger and larger elderly population. Frankly, the future looks ominous for our children who will grow up as part of the too small workforce. And, as demographer Joel Kotkin has been pointing out for years, and as we mentioned earlier, "A society that is increasingly single and childless is likely to be more concerned with serving current needs than addressing the future-oriented requirements of children. Since older people vote more than younger ones, and children have no say at all, political power could shift toward non-childbearing people."[11]

2. It will undermine our societal motivation and gradually decrease our productivity and abundance.

As pointed out by Nick Schulz in his book *Home Economics: The Consequences of Changing Family Structure,* falling birthrates can affect entrepreneurialism because young people are such a driving force. Society, in turn, could lose its "dynamism" in the areas of culture, economics, and technology.[12] Also, as mentioned earlier, statistics consistently show that married people with children earn more, save more, and spend more than single individuals.

3. It will make our living patterns less economical and more wasteful.

Living together as families is a much more efficient way to live than one person to a house. In some cities, a majority of homes are now occupied by one single individual. Stockholm, Sweden, is an example, where 60 percent of households have only one resident.[13]

There are no economies of scale in this kind of situation—just try to imagine the Swedish government attempting to meet welfare and medical needs as the population ages. Its only alternative will be raising taxes even more as that 60 percent needs care and lacks the family structure that could provide it.

4. It will change our outlook and our collective character, pushing us into more self-focused attitudes and paradigms that do not bode well for the broader society.

It is through the responsibility and sacrifice of marriage and parenting that we develop many parts of our morality and our character. We quoted David Brooks of the *New York Times* earlier, but the quote deserves repeating here: "People are not better off when they are given maximum personal freedom to do what they want. They're better off when they are enshrouded in commitments that transcend personal choice—commitments to family, God, craft, and country."[14]

5. It will result in increasing numbers of people who are missing out on life's greatest joys.

This is just our personal opinion, of course. But as detailed previously, the National Marriage Project from the University of Virginia does offer evidence that married people, with or without children, have significantly less depression than singles; and 57 percent of married women with children felt their life had an important purpose, while only 40 percent of women without children felt the same.

So, we are all dependent on marriage in a number of different ways. But of course, many will say, "Don't be so worried about how other people live. Let everyone choose his or her own path. What others choose won't affect me. It doesn't matter."

Well, the fact is that it does matter, and it affects everyone. Where dramatically increasing numbers of people are choosing not to marry and not to have kids, it not only robs them of their best chance for long-term growth and happiness, but it also robs all of us of the dream of living in an improving, progressing society where children can grow up with as much or more potential and as many opportunities as we had.

Another Pew Research Study on the family carries within it a disturbing paradox: It shows that Americans continue to revere and recognize the importance of family yet increasingly believe that marriage is becoming obsolete. Marriage, in other words, is not a necessary component of family. What a devastatingly dangerous message!

The other problem is that "family" in this new marriage-less paradigm can be any configuration of persons who care for each other and live together.

Why is that dangerous? Why is it a problem? Simply because the minute we take the commitment of marriage between a man and a woman out of the equation for family we start losing the stability, the longevity, the procreation, the self-sacrifice, the fidelity, the unconditional love, and virtually all of the other reasons for having families in the first place.

Taking a closer look at some of the key findings of the Pew Research Center:[15]

- The vast majority (76 percent) of Americans consider the family to be the most important and most satisfying element of their lives.
- Another 22 percent say that family is one of the most important elements.
- Only 1 percent say the family is not important.

But the problem, in the words of *USA Today*, is that "marriage is increasingly optional and could be on its way to obsolescence."[16]

- Marriage is declining among all groups.
- Four in ten say marriage is obsolete.
- Among twenty-five to thirty-four-year-olds, more are unmarried than married.
- 80 percent say an unmarried couple with a child is a family.
- Cohabitation (unmarried man and woman living together) has doubled since 1960.

The bottom line is that Americans are collectively confused. On the one hand, something deep inside tells people that family is the most important thing and that an essential element of family is commitment. And folks know instinctively what is best for kids and for society. According to Pew Research Center, 61 percent say that kids need both a father and a mother to grow up happily and seven in ten say that the trend toward more single mothers is bad for society.[17]

> The best thing you can do for the institution of marriage is to work on your own marriaging.

Yet on the other hand, many of these same people turn around and say that people don't necessarily need marriage to be a family. Essentially, Americans recognize the importance of commitment, but don't like to give it a name—like *marriage*.

Somehow the most obvious connections seem to fly right over our collective consciousness. We know family is important. We know families that break up cause tremendous individual problems and societal problems. We know that more families are breaking up than ever before. We know that cohabiting partners are more likely to break up than married couples. Yet we seem content to let marriage become obsolete and to naively think we can continue to uphold the importance of family without upholding the importance of marriage.

But not you! The very fact that you are reading this book is good evidence that you not only value your marriage, but value marriage in general—as an institution, as a lifestyle, and as the glue that holds this world together.

And the best thing you can do for the institution of marriage is to work on your own marriaging. Be deliberate and vocal about your love for and support for this marvelously true thing that makes our lives more worthy of living and that underpins the future for all of us.

Afterword:

A PERSONAL AFFIRMATION
FROM THE EYRES

THE VIEW FROM HERE

(LOOKING FORWARD AND BACK AFTER FIFTY YEARS.)

On the very day this book releases, we celebrate our golden wedding anniversary. Fifty years! And the view from here is remarkably clear.

At this stage, we see vividly that the most valuable things in our lives—far and away the most valuable—are our relationships, specifically our family relationships, and most particularly our marriage partnership.

"Mawwiage is what bwings us togevah today" is a line from our favorite movie, *The Princess Bride.*

And indeed, marriage is the one thing that can bring us together today, and the one thing that can bring the world together.

The picture on the previous page—which has become our logo in recent years, appearing at the top or bottom of all our columns, articles, or podcasts, as well as in our books and speaking introductions—is special to us for several reasons. Let us each share some:

Richard: The picture works because Linda is behind but above me. Looking back, I can see how she has been behind everything I've done even as she is always above me in the qualities and attributes of who she is.

Linda: The granite wall behind us is the granite wall of the temple where we took our marriage vows "for time and for all eternity" fifty years ago. Granite is the strongest of stone.

Richard: I like that we are smiling. In fact, I'm laughing! We've learned that we each have more control over each other's happiness than over our own. And together, we can smile even at things that might crush us separately.

Linda: I'm glad that we are wearing our coats. Marriage is a cloak and a warmth-giver, and the kind of bundling-together that happens over the years actually makes it a joy to grow older together.

Think of yourselves as a couple. What is your favorite picture together? What does it show? What does it make you feel as you look at it?

Marriage and family are the *end*, and everything else is the *means*.

What are you creating? Does the relationship you are working on get as much time, as much priority, as much planning, and as much mental energy as the career you are working on, or the education, or the resume, or even the parenting?

Take our word for it. From this vantage point or this time-won perspective, other things—all other things—pale in comparison to the beauty and meaning of familial commitment and love. Accomplishments don't hold a candle to relationships. Material possessions are only the props that may help family flourish. And every other interest, everything we have ever worked for, produces its full joy only when it is shared within our marriage.

Marriage and family are the *end*, and everything else is the *means*. That seems so obvious to us now, but it was harder to see earlier on. One reason we chose to write this book is because we hope to help you realize this sooner, or be reassured in the realization that your spouse—despite the rough roads you've seen—should be the most vital and valuable thing, the most important part of your life, and the source of your greatest fulfillment and joy.

So, take that much from us. Don't rediscover the wheel or think that the only way to know for yourself what matters most is to try everything and see. If you are married, we hope reading this book will make your marriage better. If you are cohabitating but not married, view this book as a motivation to marry. If you are living single, use this book as a provocative challenge that there is something better—and contemplate if you might want to spend more time and effort seeking it.

Because here is the thing: You can't develop into your fullest, best self by yourself. As the French say, "*On peut tout gagné dans le solitude sauf le character.*" You can gain everything in solitude except for your character.

The commitment of marriage is both the path and the measurement of who you truly are—at your deepest core—and of things you could never discover or become on your own.

As for us . . .

We love marriage.

We love the partnership of marriage.

We love the romance of marriage.

We love the excitement of marriage.

We love the commitment of marriage.

We love the challenge of marriage.

We love the security of marriage.

We love the synergy of marriage.

We love the sacrifice of marriage.

We love the institution of marriage—the oldest institution in the world and the union that makes all other unions possible and stable.

Can other institutions, countries, governments, churches, communities, or neighborhoods flourish without the most basic unit, the most personal and fundamental union, the most fundamental human connection and commitment of all—that of marriage?

It is doubtful. Take away the most basic bond, and you take away the glue that holds everything together. Instead of structure, stability, and predictability in the institutions of a society, you get random, erratic moving parts that can work against instead of for the common good.

A PRIVATE WORD FROM RICHARD

Let me speak by myself for a moment so I can say some personal things about Linda. I originally wrote this in an article during the week that falls in between Linda's birthday and Mother's Day. It was an opportunity to voice some things about marriage and mothers as well as other things to Linda and to anyone reading them.

First of all, I love having someone with whom I share everything and who knows everything about me, sometimes things I don't even know myself.

I love partnership with my wife, full and total partnership where we literally try to share everything—even bank accounts, even our emails, even everything—and where there are no secrets, not even little ones.

Neither of us is anything remotely close to perfect, and neither is our relationship. But I love the synergy of that and how all of my weaknesses seem to be made up and compensated for by Linda's strengths, and where, on our best days, our total is greater than the sum of its parts.

I love that we each have our own ways of doing things, very different ways that, again on our good days, complement each other and make possible things that neither of us could do on our own.

I have come to acknowledge and partially understand that Linda is, like all women, a complex organism and that if I try to change one little thing or one little part of her then I might set off some kind of chain reaction that would alter the whole and end up changing the very things I love most about her. Therefore, I tell her—in total honesty—that I would not change one little thing about her. I have told her that so much, and explained the reasoning behind it, that I think she finally believes me.

> **I love the word *husband*. It means stewardship; it means care; it means cherishing and taking care of.**

I love the word *husband*. It means stewardship; it means care; it means cherishing and taking care of. But I think it also means partnership—the kind with complete respect and unbending commitment and fidelity.

I love that Linda's role in our family is the most important one—
that her instinctive and intuitive love of our children has guided
their lives more than any other thing and that the title of Mother
truly is the most important, influential, indispensable, and irreplace-
able role on this planet.

A PRIVATE WORD FROM LINDA

In response to Richard's private message, I must start by saying that
never in my wildest dreams could I have imagined a happier, more
adventurous, more chaotic, more fulfilling life than the one I lucked
out with when I married Richard Eyre.

It was a hard decision to give up my dreams of traveling through
Europe before I made the commitment to be tied down to marriage
and children. After Richard's first attempt to get me to say "yes" I
delivered a definite "no"; back when we were mere babes in college,
I had a firm conviction that I should not get married until I was
twenty-eight! I stuck to my dream of traveling for two more years
(until I was twenty-two) before finally admitting to myself that he
was "the one." Little did I know that I would be traveling to more
than one hunderd countries with him, often with a gaggle of children in tow. In addition, besides exploring the world with the kids,
we'd be speaking to parents and families about how important their
work is in saving the world, one family at a time!

What a grand adventure it has been to be married to the aston-
ishing Richard Eyre! I must admit there are just a few tiny things
that I *would* like him to change, but I've given up hope and decided
that I love him in spite of—and maybe because of—those strange
idiosyncrasies!

I would love to watch a private movie of our fifty years together,
starting with our marriage in its infancy. It would be so fun to see us
driving across the country on our honeymoon to begin our new life

in Boston where Richard would be attending the Harvard Business School and I would be teaching music at a nearby junior high school.

It was August and the drive was eventful. We had basically no money and were saving pennies whenever we could. The highlights (or should I say lowlights) included a surprise awakening after a peaceful sleep in a park somewhere in the Midwest by the lawn sprinklers set to start at five o'clock in the morning. A wild scramble ensued, with a lot of screaming from me and laughing from Richard, as we gathered sleeping bags and pillows, hoping they would be dry by the next night.

Most of our dining during that trip was at McDonald's, sharing Big Macs and fries as we traveled through the endless miles of wheat fields in the Midwest, and up into the Northeast, finally reaching Niagara Falls (in our minds, the honeymoon Shangri-la). A pretty funny scene in our movie would be to see us riding the elevator to the top of the observation tower to view the spectacular falls from above and then deciding that we should splurge and spend just enough money to share one meal at the elegant restaurant at the top. After a long wait to get in and poring over the menu for quite a while, we decided to share an entrée that we could afford. We were totally miffed—and quite humiliated—when the waiter informed us that we had to either order two meals or leave. I guess other starving honeymooners had tried the same thing and the management had decided to put an end to it. We left.

The movie would include years of struggling to build our family and our businesses. It would include summers full of crazy adventures; when we began to write in earnest, we could spend our summers wherever we could find paper and pens. One audacious summer was spent building a log cabin from scratch in the wilderness of Oregon, teaching the kids how to work and love nature. We spent many summers with all the kids in a tiny cabin near my hometown in Idaho at Bear Lake, practicing music with the kids with a pretty modicum amount of success. There was a summer in the very foreign but incredible culture of Japan and another one in Romania. And there were years of book tours and speaking tours filled with funny experiences for Richard and I, and wild adventures on humanitarian expeditions to Bolivia, Africa, Mexico, and India with the kids.

It is such a good exercise to look back to see how far we've come as well as to look forward at what we still want to accomplish.

Watching that movie would probably make us laugh at our immaturity and our naivety. It would make us wonder why it took us so long to figure out how to resolve our issues with each other without staying up all night. Or laugh at how many times we would have to fail and try again as we worked through our different ways of viewing the world.

From our current (aging) perspective, we would probably marvel at how we did some of the things we did and how we survived with nine kids. We would want to see the hard times as well as the good ones and hopefully it would help us put into perspective some of the things we missed. In the frenzy we might regret that we didn't spend more time relishing our lives together or wish we had paid more attention to a child who needed something we didn't see. Hopefully, we would see very clearly in retrospect the overwhelming importance of love.

What would the movie of your marriage be like? Whether you are just starting your marriage or getting near the home stretch, the most striking similarity is that every marriage is different. It is such a good exercise to look back to see how far we've come as well as to look forward at what we still want to accomplish in the greatest and most important relationship challenge of our lives: marriage!

A FINAL WORD FROM BOTH OF US

One thing we tried very hard not to do in this book is to assume or
to presume.

We don't assume that your relationship is just like ours; we don't
presume that our goals and hopes for our marriage are exactly like
yours. We know that there are no one-size-fits-all solutions or quick
fixes for marriage. We know that your situation, your personalities,
your pressures, and your expectations are completely unique, and
we don't hold any of ours up as the ideal or the preferred.

But another thing we know is that *none* of us gives our marriage
the full effort and attention it deserves. Because of its profound effect
on everything else in our lives, marriage deserves *every* effort. And
attention is the very point. We want this book, and the ideas in it, to
get your attention, to help you think more about your marriage and
about what that marriage can become.

The more attention you give this greatest relationship, the
more likely you will be to find your own unique channels and your
own made-just-for-you methods and approaches. In doing so,
you can start to move—not always steadily and often in fits and
starts—toward the best that your own unique, particular, peculiar,
one-of-a-kind marriage can be.

We hope that one result of your reading this book will be that
you begin—right now—to prioritize your marriage above everything else. That sounds like a pretty big demand, but we have come
to realize, both through our experience and our observation, that
couples who make their marriage the single most important thing
in their lives cannot fail. Learn to think of your partnership not just
as the means to other wonderful ends, but as an end in itself—as the
end you want all else to lead to.

One final parting shot and a bit of a warning: *Get rid of guilt.* It
is natural, when we think of familial relationships, to realize places

where we could have done better, times when we let someone down, or moments when we missed a need or were too aware of ourselves and not aware enough of our

One final parting shot and a bit of a warning: *Get rid of guilt.*

partner or our children. We blame ourselves for mistakes that have been made and for bad things that have happened. But relationships are not a game of perfect, and the problem with guilt is that it makes relationships even less perfect. Guilt leads to feelings of failure, and failure is self-fulfilling and self-perpetuating.

> **Richard:** *We were on a road trip on a Sunday and happened to visit a small rural church along our route. By coincidence, the Sunday School class we ended up in was having a discussion on marriage and parenting. Most of the people there looked like regular farm folk, but there was one other visitor who looked out of place. He was in a three-piece suit, and this guy had all the answers. His marriage was perfect and he told the class why; his kids were perfect—his daughter the valedictorian and his son the student body president—and he told us why; he had no problems and told us how he did it. After the fifth or sixth time he raised his hand to give yet another "answer," the class was feeling a little oppressed. A short, unimposing farmer raised his hand, turned to face the big bragger, and said, "Excuse me, sir, but God must not have thought too much of you as a husband and a father, giving you all them easy kids and that perfect marriage."*
>
> *I gave Linda's hand a squeeze and whispered "Amen."*

The fact is that each of our marriages and each of our family situations are different—and none of them are easy, and all of us have made mistakes. So, no guilt! Instead, just know (or just assume, or just take our word for it), that you did the best you could with what you knew and what you were capable of at the time. Let's close this book in a guilt-free zone, where we all look for how to do a little bit better and where we focus on the future of our relationships, not on the past.

We were at a friend's house once and noticed a fairly thick book on the coffee table titled *The Joys of Growing Older*. We opened it and felt a mixture of disappointment and mirth to find that all the pages were blank.

We were thinking about that book as we sat down together to start writing this book. It occurred to us that one approach we could take would be to have only two pages of this volume with anything printed on them. The first page could say COMMITMENT and the second one could say LOVE.

Then the rest of the book could be blank pages, because couples who get those two things right, who never let up on either, and who keep deepening both, these are the couples whose marriages cannot fail—whose unions continue to grow and get sweeter.

If we wanted to take that two-page book to an even deeper level, we could add one modifying word to each of the two pages so that they read TOTAL COMMITMENT and LOVE MORE.

When commitment is without condition and without caveat or exception it becomes a warm blanket of security and safety that maximizes the confidence and capacity of both spouses and that makes all differences or friction become opportunities for growth and synergy.

When commitment is without condition and without caveat or exception it becomes a warm blanket of security and safety.

Commitment is not something you do later, after you are sure you are compatible; it is the thing you do sooner, to maximize your chance of becoming compatible. Real commitment must be developed and constantly deepened over time, and to become real, it must be frequently *expressed.*

As love keeps multiplying, growing, and finding more avenues of insight and expression it becomes a dynamic, adventurous, living thing that is filled with excitement and that moves in the opposite direction of ruts or boredom. We like the phrase "love more" better than the phrase "more love" because we like the word "love" to be a verb rather than a noun.

Consider that the spouse who lives and sleeps and eats and parents or grandparents with you every day may be by far your greatest asset, blessing, gift, resource, and friend. Let each other's characteristics and idiosyncrasies become endearing rather than annoying and draw you closer together rather than pull you apart. Fight the tendency to take your spouse for granted. Develop your ability to adore and cherish. Define your own oneness and pursue it romantically. Understand that romance only dies when we fail to nourish it. Live for love.

APPENDIX A:
A SHORT Q&A WITH
SUCCESS MAGAZINE

An interview we did with a national magazine captures and briefly summarizes some of the directions of this book:[1]

Family and relationship experts Linda and Richard Eyre have coauthored more than 30 books, including *New York Times* #1 bestselling *Teaching Your Children Values* and *The Book of Nurturing*, and have been frequent guests on *Oprah, Good Morning America, CBS This Morning*, and *Today*. Married for nearly fifty years, they have raised nine children. They describe each year as "better than the last." *Success* sat down with the Eyres to learn how they keep the magic alive.

SM: Is there a secret to a lasting marriage?

Yes, and it is one word: commitment. *The stronger the commitment, the better the chance a marriage will have in enduring the challenges and buffering the conflicts that all marriages experience. The commitment must be strong enough that bailing out is never an option.*

SM: How can couples keep the romance alive with the frenetic schedule of kids, work, upkeep of the house, and errands?

Two thoughts on this one: First, continue the courtship. We try to go on a date every Friday night. We have done that since we were married. If something else is scheduled on Friday, we shift our date to another night of the week. We go alone—just the two of us—we talk, we share, we express love in the same romantic ways we did when we first fell in love. Things like flowers, poetry, and spontaneous surprises can be involved. Once a month, our date is called a "five-facet review" because we go to a restaurant and spend the entire evening brainstorming about each of our kids. How is Josh doing physically? Mentally? Emotionally? Socially? Spiritually? We take notes. We always hit upon a couple of key areas to concentrate on during the month ahead, and we nip problems in the bud. Working together on our greatest stewardship—our kids—draws us closer together as a couple and as a partnership.

Second, we have a weekly Sunday Session, as we call it. It's our planning and scheduling time when we work out the week ahead, and it also includes what we call testimonies, when we both take five minutes or so and express our feelings for each other, for life, for the kids. It's like a weekly formal re-declaration of our love and commitment to each other.

SM: How can married couples improve communication?

Sunday Sessions and weekly dates help a lot, but we are both amazingly strong-willed and opinionated. It is at times when we disagree, which is frequently, that we need our best communication. We have what we call the paraphrase-back rule—before one of us can make the next point or argument, he or she must first paraphrase or repeat back the point just made by the other to their satisfaction. Then we can make our next point. This defuses disagreements pretty fast and improves the quantity and quality of empathy, which is the most important tool in a marriage.

It's not about never disagreeing; it's about how we handle disagreements. Disagreement, well-handled, is what produces marriage synergy.

SM: What are some of the common ways couples begin to drift apart, and how can they get back on the same path?

If there are not regular, scheduled times to be together and to communicate and plan together, drifting is guaranteed to happen.

Another way we try to stay on the same page is to think of our relationship as two very important and equal limited partnerships. The "inner partnership" is all about the kids, the house, and all that goes on inside. The "outer partnership" is about the businesses, the finances, and the causes we are involved in outside the home. In each case, it is the responsibility of the general partner to keep the limited partner completely informed and up to date, and it is the job of the limited partner to stay involved and maintain an equal partnership.

We are fortunate that, in our case, as we write books together, additional coordination, communication and synergy always take place.

By the way, it is not a bad idea to do a little writing together in any marriage—to write up a little document of your parenting philosophy and of your communication techniques. Coauthoring things, even private documents, draws people together.

SM: Money is one of the most argued topics in marriages. How can couples harmoniously manage money in a marriage?

Share everything. Have no secrets. Have joint, not separate, bank accounts. Plan together. Make finances a part of the Sunday Sessions and the weekly dates.

SM: What are the best ways couples can keep magic in a marriage?

You have to work at magic! The best way we know is to actually set relationship goals. Most people set goals only for their achievements and accomplishments, such as career goals, money goals, and weight-loss goals. It doesn't occur to many that we can have relationship goals because relationships are too hard to quantify or to measure. But, in fact, a goal is a clear vision of how you want something to be in the future. So, we both make relationship goals by writing a description of our relationship five years out. We each do this separately, and we do not share the descriptions with each other. These represent our ideas of what our ideal relationship could be, and instead of waiting for the other person to do something about it, we both work at it in our own way, reading the description or relationship goal often, as each of us unilaterally tries to bring the relationship closer to that ideal.

SM: If a couple is contemplating separation, how would you advise them to reconsider?

View separation as a last resort. Think of it as amputation—something to not even consider until all other options and remedies are tried. When you have an infection or some kind of a dysfunctional malady, you try to heal it or cure it first. You cut it off only when all else fails.

The first thing we would prescribe is a relationship restructure, wherein proactive steps are taken to rebuild the relationship from the ground up. The tools would be the five-years-out relationship description, the weekly Sunday Sessions, the Friday date night and the monthly five-facet review mentioned earlier.

Too many relationships just become what they are through neglect and reactivity. Make yours what you want it to be through attention and being proactive. Bottom line: The magic comes from hard, mental work.

SM: It seems almost inexplicable that, as *New York Times* #1 bestselling authors on family, you have waited until now—until your fiftieth wedding anniversary—to write your first and only book on marriage.

Actually, it's totally explicable. It took us fifty years to figure it out for ourselves.

APPENDIX B:
BOOK GROUP QUESTIONS

1. Why do you think the Eyres decided to approach the subject of marriage from the myths—from the un-truth side?
2. Would you have put the myths in the same order that the Eyres did? What do you think was their reason for putting the Clone Myth first? Why did they put the Demise Myth last?
3. Which myth was most obviously a myth to you—most easy to recognize as something that is not true and that needs replacing? And which of the myths did you initially want to defend as truths?
4. Which of the myths has done the most damage in your own marriage?
5. Are there any of the myths that you still believe, despite what you have read in this book?
6. Would you recommend this book to a friend whose marriage is on the rocks? Would you recommend it to a friend who seems to have a great marriage that needs little help?
7. Before reading the book, would you have said that you generally prioritized achievements over relationships? If so, has this book changed your mind?

8. Do you think that you could "joyfully, completely, enthusi-
    astically" give up your independence in favor of an interde-
    pendence with your spouse?

9. What do you think about the difference between oneness
    and equality in marriage? Which one appeals to you most?

10. In what ways have you tried to fix your spouse? How have
    those efforts worked out?

11. What was your reaction to the Perfection Myth? Do you
    believe that we each have a soul mate that we should be
    trying to find?

12. Do the Eyres overstate the importance of commitment and
    portray it as a panacea that will get us through anything?

13. What are your biggest personal take-aways from this book?
    What adjustments will you make in your own thinking and
    try to make in your marriage relationship?

NOTES

Chapter 1:

1. McGuire, M. "Michelle Obama's Advice for a Lasting Marriage: Get Help When You Need It." *Institute for Family Studies*. November 15, 2018. https://ifstudies.org/blog/michelle-obamas-advice-for-a-lasting-marriage-get-help-when-you-need-it. See also https://www.youtube.com/watch?v=zDBb88MOYuQ

Chapter 2:

1. The National Marriage Project. http://nationalmarriageproject.org

Chapter 3:

1. Brooks, D. "The Age of Possibility." *New York Times*. November 15, 2012. https://www.nytimes.com/2012/11/16/opinion/brooks-the-age-of-possibility.html

2. MacDonald, G. "Quotable Quote." *Goodreads*. https://www.goodreads.com/quotes/905333-the-love-of-our-neighbor-is-the-only-door-out

3. Bruce Feiler, *The First Love Story: Adam, Eve, and Us*. New York: Penguin Press, 2017.

Chapter 4:

1. Cohn, D. "Love and Marriage." *Pew Research Center—Social and Demographic Trends*. February 13, 2013. http://www.pewsocialtrends.org/2013/02/13/love-and-marriage/

Chapter 5:

1. "100 Funny Jokes and Quotes about Love, Sex and Marriage." *The Telegraph*. December 14, 2018. https://www.telegraph.co.uk/comedy/comedians/100-funny-jokes-quotes-love-sex-marriage/will-ferrell/)

2. Beecher, H.W. "Quotable Quote." *Goodreads*. https://www.goodreads.com/quotes/796384-a-person-without-a-sense-of-humor-is-like-a

3. Hope, B. "Bob Hope Quotes about Laughter." *AZ Quotes*. https://www.azquotes.com/author/6880-Bob_Hope/tag/laughter

4. Brittle, Z. "H Is for Humor." *The Gottman Institute.* April 14, 2014. https://www.gottman.com/blog/h-is-for-humor/

5. Parrott, L., and L. Parrott. "Bringing Laughter into Your Marriage." *Focus on the Family.* https://www.focusonthefamily.com/marriage/daily-living/humor-in-marriage/bringing-laughter-into-your-marriage

Chapter 6:

1. Brigham Young University. "Couples Who Delay Having Sex Get Benefits Later, Study Suggests." *ScienceDaily.* December 29, 2010. https://www.science-daily.com/releases/2010/12/101222112102.htm

2. Regnerus, M. and J. Uecker. *Premarital Sex in America: How Young Americans Meet, Mate, and Think about Marrying.* Oxford: Oxford University Press, 2011.

3. Nugent, C. N., and Daugherty, J. "A Demographic, Attitudinal, and Behavioral Profile of Cohabiting Adults in the United States, 2011–2015." *National Health Statistics Reports.* https://www.cdc.gov/nchs/data/nhsr/nhsr111.pdf

4. Rosenfeld, M. J. and K. Roesler. "Cohabitation Experience and Cohabitation's Association With Marital Dissolution." *Wiley Online Library.* https://onlineli-brary.wiley.com/doi/full/10.1111/jomf.12530

5. Carroll, J. S. "Slow but Sure: Does the Timing of Sex during Dating Matter?" *Institute for Family Studies.* August 14, 2014. https://ifstudies.org/blog/slow-but-sure-does-the-timing-of-sex-during-dating-matter/

6. The Eyre Family. https://www.theeyrefamily.com

7. Eyre, R. and L. "Mormon Parenting: Charity on the law of chastity." *Desert News.* https://www.deseretnews.com/article/865566867/Charity-on-the-law-of-chastity.html

Chapter 7:

1. Genesis 2:24, KJV

2. Mark 10:9, KJV

3. 1 Corinthians 11:11, KJV

4. Matthew 10:17, KJV

5. "Christian views on marriage." *Wikipedia.* https://en.wikipedia.org/wiki/Christian_views_on_marriage

6. Hebrews 13:4, KJV

7. "Christian views on marriage." *Wikipedia*. https://en.wikipedia.org/wiki/
Christian_views_on_marriage

Chapter 8:

1. Finkel, E. J. "Preface." *The All-or-Nothing Marriage: How the Best Marriages
Work*. New York: Dutton, 2017.

2. Kotkin, J. *The Rise of Post-familialism: Humanity's Future?* Civil Service
College–Singapore, Chapman University, and Fieldstead and Company, 2012.

3. Brooks, D. "The Age of Possibility." *New York Times*. November 15, 2012.
https://www.nytimes.com/2012/11/16/opinion/brooks-the-age-of-possibility.
html

4. Reeves, R. V. "How to Save Marriage in America." The Atlantic. February
13, 2014. https://www.theatlantic.com/business/archive/2014/02/
how-to-save-marriage-in-america/283732/

5. The National Marriage Project. *Reports*. http://nationalmarriageproject.org/
reports/

6. Donovan, C., W. B. Wilcox, and P. Taylor. "When Marriage Disappears:
The Retreat from Marriage in Middle America." *The Heritage Foundation*.
February 22, 2011. https://www.heritage.org/marriage-and-family/report/
when-marriage-disappears-the-retreat-marriage-middle-america

7. "The Decline of Marriage and Rise of New Families." *Pew
Research Center—Social and Demographic Trends*. November
18, 2010. https://www.pewsocialtrends.org/2010/11/18/
the-decline-of-marriage-and-rise-of-new-families/2/#ii-overview

8. Porter, E. "Maybe We're not Robbing the Cradle." *New York Times*. April 10,
2005. https://www.nytimes.com/2005/04/10/weekinreview/maybe-were-not-
robbing-the-cradle.html

9. Schultz, N. *Home Economics: The Consequences of Changing Family Structure*.
Washington, DC: AEI Press, 2013.

10. "Most US Adults Are Now Single, in Major Shift." *NBC News*. https://www.
nbclosangeles.com/news/national-international/Single-Now-Make-up-Over-
Half-of-the-US-Adult-Population-274692871.html

11. Kotkin, J. *The Rise of Post-familialism: Humanity's Future?* Civil Service College–Singapore, Chapman University, and Fieldstead and Company, 2012.

12. Schultz, N. *Home Economics: The Consequences of Changing Family Structure.* Washington, DC: AEI Press, 2013.

13. Klinenberg, E. "One's a Crowd." *New York Times.* February 4, 2012. https://www.nytimes.com/2012/02/05/opinion/sunday/living-alone-means-being-social.html

14. Brooks, D. "The Age of Possibility." *New York Times.* November 15, 2012. https://www.nytimes.com/2012/11/16/opinion/brooks-the-age-of-possibility.html

15. "The Decline of Marriage and Rise of New Families." *Pew Research Center—Social and Demographic Trends.* November 18, 2010. https://www.pewsocialtrends.org/2010/11/18/the-decline-of-marriage-and-rise-of-new-families/2/#ii-overview

16. Jayson, S. "Nearly 40% say marriage is becoming obsolete." USA Today. https://usatoday30.usatoday.com/yourlife/sex-relationships/marriage/2010-11-18-1Amarriage18_ST_N.htm

    "4 in 10 Say Marriage Is Becoming Obsolete." *CBS News.* November 18, 2010. https://www.cbsnews.com/news/4-in-10-say-marriage-is-becoming-obsolete/

17. "The Decline of Marriage and Rise of New Families." *Pew Research Center—Social and Demographic Trends.* November 18, 2010. https://www.pewsocialtrends.org/2010/11/18/the-decline-of-marriage-and-rise-of-new-families/2/#ii-overview

Appendix A:

1. *Success Magazine* interview on "Making Marriage Work."

ABOUT THE AUTHORS

Linda and Richard Eyre (who are releasing this book on their fiftieth wedding anniversay) are *New York Times* #1 bestselling authors whose writing career has spanned four decades and whose books have sold in the millions. They have appeared together on virtually all major national talk shows, including *Oprah* and *Today,* and have seen their books translated into a dozen languages. They do a weekly podcast, *Eyres on the Road,* and currently spend most of their time traveling and speaking to audiences throughout the world on families, parenting, and life-balance (and trying to keep up with their thirty-one [and counting] grandchildren). The Eyres' vision statement is "Fortify families by celebrating commitment, popularizing parenting, bolstering balance, validating values, and glorifying grandparenthood."

Please follow the Eyres on Instagram @richardlindaeyre and on valuesparenting.com.

OTHER FAMILIUS BOOKS
BY THE EYRES

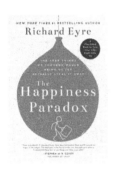

THE HAPPINESS PARADOX: The Very Things We Thought Would Bring Us Joy Actually Steal It Away

Richard contends that the three things today's society desires the most—control, ownership, and independence—are, paradoxically, the three things that bring the most challenges and unhappiness in our lives. Read this book from one side for the problem of the paradox, and then read it from the other side for the solution of the paradigm.

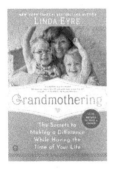

GRANDMOTHERING: The Secrets to Making a Difference While Having the Time of Your Life

Linda shares her secret formula for teaching your grandchildren values, building meaningful connections with them, and giving them grit and resilience, plus an appendix of easy recipes to feed a crowd.

BEING A PROACTIVE GRANDFATHER: How to Make a Difference

Richard Eyre encourages those of us whose children have had children to ask ourselves a very important question: "what kind of grandfather will you be?" The two key words in the title are BEING and GRAND. A great book for grandmothers to give to their husbands!

POEMS: About Family and Favorites: Exploring Who and What We Love

Here, for the first time in published form, Richard Eyre shares some of his most poetic efforts for those who have enjoyed his prose, and for those who haven't. None who know Richard will be surprised that most of his poems connect to family.

TENNIS AND LIFE: 30 Winning Lessons for the Two Greatest Games

Bestselling author and tennis champion Richard Eyre explains why, of all sports, tennis is the best metaphor for life. He then shares thirty principles that will help you enjoy both games more—and play both games better.

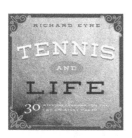

THE HALF-DIET DIET: The Guaranteed Weight-Loss Program That Reboots Your Body, Mind, and Spirit for a Happier Life

More than just a weight-loss program, *The Half-Diet Diet* helps you meet your weight-loss goals by taming your physical, mental, and spiritual appetites. The Eyres' promise: "The weight you lose will be the least of the rewards that appetite-control will bring."

THE THANKFUL HEART: How Deliberate Gratitude Can Change Every Texture of Our Lives

In this beautifully illustrated book, we find the opportunity to consciously and deliberately develop our own skill to feel gratitude more deeply, and give it more freely. As the Eyres say, "Gratitude does not lead to happiness, gratitude IS happiness in its most obtainable form.

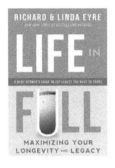

LIFE IN FULL: Maximizing Your Longevity and Legacy

A seven-question blueprint for how to spend the next twenty years living the life you have always wanted and enjoying the life fulfillment you deserve. This is a book written for Baby Boomers who want to make the "Autumn" of their lives their best season, and who want to prioritize family relationships more than ever before.

THE TURNING: Why the State of the Family Matters, and What the World Can Do About It

In the spirit of Friedman's *The World Is Flat*, Richard and Linda Eyre examine the connections between the world's mounting social problems and the breakdown of families and look deeply at the root causes of family disintegration. Then, in the second half of the book, the Eyres suggest macro solutions for society and micro solutions and practical parenting ideas for parents inside their own homes.

By ordering directly from Familius,
you can get the Eyres' other books for 50% off!

Just visit
familius.com/eyres-special
and use the access code FamiliusFriend.

Enjoy!

ABOUT FAMILIUS

Familius is a global trade publishing company that publishes books and other content to help families be happy. We believe that the family is the fundamental unit of society and that happy families are the foundation of a happy life. We recognize that every family looks different, and we passionately believe in helping all families find greater joy. To that end, we publish books for children and adults that invite families to live the Familius Nine Habits of Happy Family Life: *love together, play together, learn together, work together, talk together, heal together, read together, eat together,* and *laugh together.* Founded in 2012, Familius is located in Sanger, California.

CONNECT

- Website: www.familius.com
- Facebook: www.facebook.com/paterfamilius
- Twitter: @familiustalk, @paterfamilius1
- Pinterest: www.pinterest.com/familius
- Instagram: @familiustalk

FAMILIUS

The most important work you ever do will be within the walls of your own home.